Barbara Wootton and the Legacy of a Pioneering Public Criminologist

This book offers an assessment of Barbara Wootton's legacy as a pioneering public criminologist. Barbara Wootton (1897–1988) was a leading British social scientist, magistrate, academic and public servant. She was also a life peer (Baroness Wootton of Abinger) and the first woman to sit on the Woolsack in the House of Lords as Deputy Speaker. One of the Royal Commissions on which she served was on the Penal System (1964) and two of the Departmental Committees were on the Business of the Criminal Courts (1958) and Criminal Statistics (1963). Of her written work, perhaps the most famous is *Social Science and Social Pathology* (published in 1959), which was an attempt to discover what the social sciences had to say about criminality, its causes and its social effects.

This book examines her career in historical context, and her contribution to thinking and scholarship on a range of topics. These topics range from the courts and the penal system and her report on the Community Service Order, to crime and criminal law and her analysis of the notions of mens rea, to her work on psychiatry and criminal justice. It explores her contribution as a Utilitarian critic in criminology, within the British empiricist tradition.

Written in a clear and direct style, this book will appeal to students and scholars of criminology, sociology, criminal justice, law and all those interested in learning more about Barbara's life and times.

Philip Bean was formerly a probation officer in the Inner London Probation and After Care Service (until 1970) before taking up appointments for the Medical Research Council. He was appointed Lecturer and Senior Lecturer at the University of Nottingham before moving to the University of Loughborough to be Director of the Midlands Centre for Criminology and Criminal Justice. He was Secretary and later President of the British Society of Criminology, and an Associate of the General Medical Council, sitting on their Fitness to Practice and Health panels. He is now Emeritus Professor of Criminology and Criminal Justice at the University of Loughborough. He is the author/editor of more than 30 books and of numerous papers in learned journals, mainly on mental disorder, crime and drugs.

Routledge Key Thinkers in Criminology
Edited by Tom Daems, *University of Leuven*
Kelly Hannah-Moffat, *University of Toronto Mississauga*
Shadd Maruna, *University of Manchester*
Tim Newburn, *London School of Economics and Political Science*

The more a discipline matures and develops the more interesting it becomes to document and reflect upon its history – including its key figures. The history of criminology includes a set of key thinkers who have defined the subject, renewed its theory and refined its methodology.

The volumes in this series are stand-alone introductions and critical examinations of the life and work of key thinkers in criminology. These volumes collectively contribute to writing and rewriting criminology's history by adding a distinctive line of inquiry: the focus on the ideas of some of the most inspiring figures from its past.

Michel Foucault
Mariana Valverde

Edwin H. Sutherland
David Friedrichs, Isabel Schoultz and Aleksandra Jordanoska

Barbara Wootton and the Legacy of a Pioneering Public Criminologist
Philip Bean

For more information about this series, please visit: www.routledge.com/Routledge-Key-Thinkers-in-Criminology/book-series/RKTC

Barbara Wootton and the Legacy of a Pioneering Public Criminologist

Philip Bean

Routledge
Taylor & Francis Group
LONDON AND NEW YORK

First published 2021
by Routledge
2 Park Square, Milton Park, Abingdon, Oxon OX14 4RN

and by Routledge
52 Vanderbilt Avenue, New York, NY 10017

Routledge is an imprint of the Taylor & Francis Group, an informa business

British Library Cataloguing-in-Publication Data
A catalogue record for this book is available from the British Library

Library of Congress Cataloging-in-Publication Data
A catalog record for this book has been requested

ISBN: 978-0-367-25396-7 (hbk)
ISBN: 978-0-429-28758-9 (ebk)

Typeset in Goudy
by Apex CoVantage, LLC

Contents

	Preface	vi
1	Barbara Wootton: her life and times	1
2	Social pathology, the courts and the penal system	26
3	Crime and the criminal law	56
4	Social work, psychiatry and criminal justice	79
5	An assessment	105
	Index	126

Preface

When it was suggested I write on Barbara Wootton's contribution to criminology for this 'Key Thinkers in Criminology' series, I gladly accepted the invitation. I knew Barbara, albeit for only a short period, but I had long been an enthusiast and a supporter of her work. I well remember reading her critique of social casework in her book *Social Science and Social Pathology*. She called it nonsense and lamentable arrogance. I heartily agreed. At the time, I was being trained as a probation officer and was expected to absorb and practise casework theory. It was a relief to know there was someone out there who understood and had the courage to say it. Later, when undertaking my own research on the application of the Mental Health Act to compulsory patients admitted to mental hospitals, it was to the writings of Barbara Wootton that I turned. I found she provided a certain clarity missing elsewhere. She saw through the subjective moral judgements that surrounded mental disorder, and she highlighted the difficulties presented to courts when dealing with the mentally disordered offender. Or, at a time in the late 1960s when the drug problem was beginning to reach epidemic proportions, it was to Barbara Wootton whose report on 'Cannabis' that I found restored some sanity to the debate. I also applauded her commitment to an empiricism in criminology which seemed to me obvious, even if at the time, that is, in the 1960s, it was being challenged by labelling theories and others.

It was not all one way. I did not share her commitment to a Utilitarian view of punishment, although as a veiled Utilitarian myself I could understand her position. Her refusal to consider an alternative such as just deserts was in my view difficult to accept. Nor did I think she was correct in her wish to dispense with the juvenile court in England and Wales and replace it with a panel system linked to the education system. And I thought she had her blind spots too; she said little about the training of probation officers, yet they too were being trained in social casework, and she must have known; she was, after all, on the Probation Advisory Committee. She also said little of female criminality, yet she was an ardent advocate of the rights of women. What of the way female offenders were being treated (literally) in prison?

But these were minor blemishes; she always wrote in a style that was entertaining. It was both cutting yet sympathetic, full of wit and humour, so that even if you thought she was wrong you could forgive her. The same was true of her private life. She was difficult to know, argumentative and prickly, at least in her later years when I knew her, but also very kind and generous.

When writing this book, I had a number of advantages. First, I could draw on an extensive and well written biography of Barbara Wootton by Ann Oakley published in 2011. Then there was an autobiography, albeit written some 20 years before Barbara died, yet still containing much that was relevant. Together, these, plus my own personal contact with Barbara, provided a considerable amount of information surrounding her life and work. Then there was her published work. Barbara Wootton was a very public figure, speaking in the House of Lords, broadcasting on radio and television, giving public lectures and publishing in learned journals, as well writing and publishing books. Also, I had written an obituary for the *British Journal of Criminology* and had jointly edited a *Festchrift*, but more importantly I edited (with Vera Seal) four volumes of Barbara's writings. I was therefore reasonably familiar with her life and work and sympathetic to her as a person. Incidentally, I found it interesting to reread the literature. I found I was additionally impressed with the range, content, style and depth of Barbara's writings. Of course, any errors or defects that are in this book are mine, whether in the content or otherwise.

It is curious that Barbara Wootton's work is rarely cited nowadays. This point was also made by her biographer, who offered various suggestions. Here, in the last chapter, I have looked at these and added to them. I am not expecting that this volume will restore Barbara Wootton's reputation, but I am hoping it will provoke sufficient interest for others to see her as an important criminologist, who offered a perspective which remains of interest. In my opinion, she deserves that, at the very least.

This book is not a biography but an account of one person's contribution to criminology. I have referred throughout to 'Barbara Wootton', occasionally calling her 'Barbara'. Although I knew her, I do not wish to convey a close relationship or a personal level beyond what it was. I have used 'Barbara' when I thought there was something more personal in what was going on and referred to her as 'Barbara Wootton' otherwise.

Also, I have written in terms which were common at the time, and following Barbara Wootton's style of writing, almost always using the male pronoun when discussing crime, and referring to 'Chairman' rather than 'Chair' or 'Chairperson' when dealing with administrative matters.

It is customary and important to acknowledge various family and friends who have helped contribute to this volume. This I gladly do, especially those who read drafts and made valuable comments. My special thanks are to Tracy Harris and Maggie Sarginson for their help and forbearance.

Philip Bean
September 2019

Chapter 1

Barbara Wootton: her life and times

Barbara Wootton (1897–1988) was a leading British social scientist, magistrate, academic and public servant. She was also a life peer (Baroness Wootton of Abinger) and the first woman to sit on the Woolsack in the House of Lords as Deputy Speaker. She was *inter alia* a member of four Royal Commissions and four Departmental Committees, a BBC Governor and a Companion of Honour.[1] She was the author of 15 books in economics and social science, and of countless published articles, with many others unpublished, the latter largely derived from her public lectures. In 1971, Barbara Wootton was hailed by the London Illustrated News as a sociologist who was 'a legend in her own lifetime', and in 1984 the BBC named her as one of 'the six women of the century'.

This is but a short summary of her many awards and achievements. And when set within the social climate in which she lived, they are additionally impressive. That is to say, she came to prominence at a time when few women reached such professional heights, and she excelled in academic subjects in which there were few shoulders on which to climb, female or otherwise. In almost every way, she broke new ground. Yet when asked as a child what she intended to do with her adult life, she answered that she would be 'an organising female with a brief case'[2] – an ambition more than achieved.

Barbara Wootton was a social scientist and a polymath. She moved easily between the various disciplines: economics, law, criminology, psychiatry, social policy and sociology. She says in her Autobiography[3] that one of her academic colleagues defined social science as 'not as much a discipline as a licence to trespass'. She approved of this definition, for trespass Barbara Wootton certainly did. She did so in such a way as to leave her own footprint, which was, to quote a distinguished professor of law, such that she made others 'think furiously about matters which they had previously taken for granted.'[4]

Barbara Wootton was very much a public social scientist. That is to say, she was someone who made her findings publicly available and someone who sought to engage the public in dialogue. She was also someone who sought to engage the experts, or specialists, in that same dialogue, but did not stay within the specialist community. She saw the task in front of her as increasing the sum total of human happiness in a strict Utilitarian sense. She did not use the term 'happiness', but she did talk of 'public good', which she saw as much the same. She expected the public good would be achieved through human intelligence and the application of scientific methods. She saw the advances made by science in the natural world and believed similar advances could be made by the application of scientific methods in the social sciences. She never faltered in this belief, although in later life she was less than hopeful about the future.

Barbara Wootton's life was dominated by two world wars, each in their different ways changing the existing social order; the first changing the certainty of Victorian values, the second changing the place of the state in public affairs. She was a committed social egalitarian; her biographer describes her as having a passion for equality.[5] Her philosophy was to place the value of human life at the centre of everything. She broadcast this message often, literally, as she appeared frequently on radio and television, and in a manner which made her a household name in Britain and elsewhere. It was a life dedicated to public service. Her interest in criminology was a logical extension of that belief.

She was born Barbara Adam, into an upper middle-class family in Cambridge in Victorian England. She had two older brothers, Neil, the eldest, and Arthur. Her parents were classical scholars, and Barbara was brought up in what she called an intellectual household. Her father, James Adam, was a Fellow and Senior Tutor at Emmanuel College, a post which he held until his premature death, aged 47. He was the only son of an Aberdeen farm worker and made his way by scholarship to Cambridge. Barbara describes him as neither remote nor austere, although very absorbed in his work. She says he was especially warm-hearted towards his students, even if sometimes merciless in his criticism of their work. Throughout his life he was troubled by fits of depression. He was said to be a brilliant teacher, so much so that Barbara believes any success she may have enjoyed as a speaker and lecturer must be largely due to qualities inherited from him.

Her mother, Adela Marion Kensington, as she was called before her marriage, was described by Barbara as an extremely intellectual woman with a strong character. Besides being a first-rate scholar, she had a good knowledge of at least three other modern languages. She was a considerable musician, being a distinguished pianist, and also sang in the Cambridge University Musical Society. Her standards were high, so much so that she found it difficult to appreciate that not everybody operated at her level or shared the same tastes and values. In politics and religion, she was conservative and conventional. Barbara describes how almost every change filled her with foreboding, and how her mother walked restlessly from room to room in anguish at the prospect that the first Old Age Pensions Act would allow old people without other means to receive a pension of as much as 5s a week.[6] Nonetheless, she was an energetic advocate of woman suffrage, though no supporter of any means involving violence and lawbreaking, as she thought these served only to postpone the day when women would get the vote.

Barbara's relations with her mother were never easy. There was, said Barbara, 'little sympathy between mother and daughter'. As with many similar childhoods, devotion to a nanny provided the emotional warmth lacking in the parental tie. It was a curious childhood, made more so by an equally curious education. Her two brothers were away at school in Winchester, both being awarded scholarships, but Barbara was educated at home, largely by her mother, until she was 13 years old. She describes her education as 'doing lessons at home' where she was expected to read a great deal for herself, chiefly English classics and English history, and later of course Greek and Roman history and literature. She also learned a lot of poetry by heart, including nearly the whole of 'Paradise Lost'. She describes her approach to learning as 'docile and industrious but not always genuinely interested'. Except for a little amateurish botany, science was totally lacking throughout her education.

At the age of 13, Barbara went as a day girl to the Perse High School in Cambridge. This was her first experience of school. Educationally, it was not very successful, largely because her precocity in certain subjects meant she was placed in a form a year or two above her age. But school did open up new horizons; for the first time, she played games and made real friends. She was close friends with two girls, one of whom she described as 'exceptionally gifted and beautiful' but who died at the age of 15. Barbara was then 14. It was not her first early experience of the death of someone close to her – her father had died when she was 10 – nor was it to be her last.

In 1914, plans were being made for her future. She was then aged 17. She describes herself as being intellectually precocious but undoubtedly very immature. It was decided she would leave school in the summer and spend two or three months in Germany living with a family and improving her German. But, as she said, 'we reckoned without the Sarajevo murders and their consequences.' So, she spent the next two years deciding what to do and in 1915 was accepted as an undergraduate at Girton College Cambridge to read economics, or rather a mixture of classics and economics, the compromise agreed to please her mother.

Her brother Arthur, a talented musician, was called up for military service immediately when war was declared. He was commissioned and reached the rank of Acting Captain. In September two years later, when he was aged 22, came the news that he was reported 'wounded and missing'. Exactly what happened no one ever knew, and his death was eventually presumed.[7]

Neil, the elder brother, was engaged in scientific research on airships but in a civilian capacity. One of Neil's friends was a certain Jack Wesley Wootton – the 'Wesley' showing the family's strong links with Methodism. Jack was the youngest son in a family of three sons and three daughters of a Nottingham lace manufacturer. Described by Barbara as 'tall, dark and handsome in a melancholy sort of way', he had been awarded a research fellowship in Cambridge, which had there been no war would have kept him there for another year. As it was, he was commissioned. He first visited the Adam household in 1915, and in the next two years his visits began to acquire a special significance. Barbara and Jack became engaged and in September 1917 were married. Jack was 26; Barbara was 20. Both were said to be 'very young for their ages'.

The wedding was planned for 5 September 1917 at the local parish church with a fortnight's honeymoon to follow. However, on the 4th of September a telegram arrived ordering Jack to service overseas. What followed is described by Barbara in her Autobiography.

> There was nothing to be done but cancel the honeymoon. One of Jack's friends discovered a farm which would be willing to take us after the wedding the next day. . . . The next afternoon we took the train to London staying overnight at the Rubens hotel. Early the following morning, a day and a half after our marriage I saw him off from Victoria (station) along with a train load of other cannon fodder. Five weeks later the War Office 'regretted to inform me' that Capt. J.W. Wootton of the 11th Battalion Suffolk Regiment had died of wounds.[8]

She adds in her Autobiography that at 49 years' distance, the emotions associated with these happenings are in the nature of things wholly spent. Not entirely, for she also says that if anyone suggests an appointment at the Rubens Hotel, she is disposed to think up an excuse for proposing an alternative meeting place.[9] In beautifully phrased passages of her Autobiography, Barbara comments thus:

> In ten years I had learned little about life much about death.
>
> Thus before I had reached my 21st birthday I had experienced the deaths of my father, my brother, my favourite school friend and the husband to whom I had been married in theory for 5 weeks and in practice for something less than 48 hours.
>
> My troubles were of course in no way unusual. What happened to me happened also in one form or another to thousands of my contemporaries; and that fact served at least to hold in check any temptation I might otherwise have had to dramatize my situation. . . . My upbringing too had left no room for self-pity; none of the adults in our family circle would ever have dreamed of using misfortune or unhappiness as an excuse for shortcomings. Whatever happened one was expected to go ahead and make the best of whatever the next job might be.

And by way of upbraiding contemporary attitudes, she says:

> In this the attitude of our elders, though somewhat exacting was, I think, much to be preferred to the contemporary practice of encouraging the young to dwell upon any early misfortunes that may have befallen them and to use these as explanations of, if not excuses for their own subsequent deficiencies. To the young it should be the future not the past that counts.

This is interesting not just for the clarity of the prose, but in a description of the values of Edwardian England. It also illustrates, or perhaps explains, much of Barbara Wootton's later critical views of those professions which place emphasis on abreaction, i.e., the pouring out of one's troubles to a practising therapist. She was particularly critical of social work – she displayed a mocking contempt of modern social work practice – and she also had a febrile scepticism of psychiatry, and an abiding interest in juvenile justice; the latter she said put too much emphasis on past events and too little on prospects for the future. She said, 'We would do better I think to encourage children from the earliest possible age, however wretched their backgrounds, to believe that they are, or at least soon will be masters of their fates.'[10]

It is difficult to know or appreciate the effect of such a dramatic loss on a young woman from a sheltered background. She says in her Autobiography that these experiences had a lasting impact on her, leaving some permanent marks on her character, and she wonders how different she would have been had things themselves been different. The death of her husband was certainly a devastating, life-changing event, rather more profound and dramatic than many others might experience in those uncertain times. She was correct to say that she was not alone, but this does not lessen the enormity of her loss. To Barbara, it directed her toward a new career and a second marriage and presumably gave further confirmation of the fragility of human relationships.

And so she went back to the first part of her undergraduate course in classics, translating English poetry into the metres of ancient Greece and Rome – not, it seems, as a resident at Girton, but to complete her academic course while living at home. She did not sit her final examination due to illness and was awarded an *aegrotat* degree. The decision to award an *aegrotat* degree was contrived with the connivance of Barbara and the medical examiner as a 'conscious and deliberate act of revenge'. It was, she says,

> revenge for the Greek verbs on my lovely summer holidays, revenge for years of being exhibited as the clever daughter, (and) revenge for a world which could value my distinction as a classical scholar above the extra hours that Jack and I could have had together.[11]

A year later, she completed the second part of her course and was awarded a degree with first class honours with distinction. She was not, however, entitled to claim a B.A. or put the letters after her name, as she was a woman. This was the first of two incidents where she was slighted by the University of Cambridge for being a woman. The second was when she was invited to give a course of lectures for one of the compulsory papers of the Economics Tripos. As a woman, she could not be a member of the university and therefore could not officially give the lectures. To solve the problem, a male economist offered to lend his name as the official lecturer, which he had no intention of giving, and there was to be a footnote saying the lectures were to be given by Barbara Wootton. 'And in those terms this ludicrous compromise did in fact appear.'[12] It was a compromise which had one unintended pleasure: as Barbara was not part of the university, she was paid for the lectures and 'for a year or two earned a great deal more money than anyone suspected or intended'.[13] Nonetheless, the incident rankled, and Barbara referred to it a number of times as examples of the way women were discriminated against.

These examples relating to her degree and the course of lectures give some indication of the personality and views of Barbara Wootton the person, and later the activist. Other than being vengeful for the time spent on Greek verbs, these are the first recorded incidents of Barbara Wootton being treated as a woman with fewer rights and privileges than a man. She later said she would not call herself a 'feminist' as this is a 'word badly abused',[14] yet she was then, and later, clearly indignant at the restrictions on women's lives. In her Autobiography, there is a chapter entitled 'Woman' which produces a litany of social failings, that is of failings to provide an equal playing field where women can compete with men.

It still remains an agenda of depressingly contemporary relevance. Her basic position was that 'men are men and women are women', but how far the apparent emotional and intellectual differences between the sexes are matters of social climate, and how far they are biologically determined, she thought, was still an open question. Whatever the differences, she said they are irrelevant when considering the type of work and profession in which a person tries to excel. It is a personal not a sexual attribute, and to follow one's calling is no more unfeminine than it is unmasculine. In Barbara's case of course, she excelled in almost everything she was called upon to undertake. She modestly says 'others broke open the doors and I walked through.'[15] Again, not strictly true; she broke open a number of doors herself.

Throughout her life, Barbara Wootton held the view that women should be equal partners with men in shaping the pattern and enjoying the fruits of our civilisation.[16] This is what we want, she said. Writing in 1967, she thought there had been a number of modest achievements, such as the increasing number of women in the professions and elsewhere. But she did not see these as evidence of that equal partnership. 'If women have come a long way we still have far to go.'[17] Although she argued persuasively for the rights of women, she was never strident, and sometimes appeared as if slightly out of touch. For example, she said 'women have to choose,' a view not commonly shared, but well in line with her pragmatic approach to human relationships.

During the interwar years she had a series of employments, first as a tutor at Girton College Cambridge, then as a Research Worker in the General Council of the Trades Union Congress of the Labour Party. This was followed by appointment as Principal of Morley College, concerned with adult education, and two years later in 1927 as Director of Studies for the extramural department of London University. It meant she worked in various university extramural departments, whether as lecturer or administrator, or a mixture of both. During this period, she was immersed in Labour Party politics and in economic questions, especially those concerned with 'the spirit of reconstruction' after World War I. She wrote and researched on economic questions such as the national debt, which was huge after the war, and about making a more just and equitable society. She worked closely with the Workers Educational Association (WEA), whose founder believed that no educated man could do harm to his community, and that education was an instrument for social justice.[18]

As far as one can see in this period of her life, she showed no active interest in other social science questions and certainly not in criminology. She was however beginning to build up a reputation for herself as a highly intelligent, competent administrator and intellectual, as well as a frequent broadcaster. She was described by her biographer as a woman young in years but with an experience and determination of much greater maturity. She was also said to make use of as many opportunities that presented themselves, but most of all would not waver from her conviction that vision, reason and hard work would make the world a more congenial and more equitable place.[19] The intellectual mould was cast in her early years, and it continued to harden throughout her life.

It was 18 years from the death of her husband Jack that she married George Wright. She describes George thus:

> Blond and vivacious, with considerable histrionic gifts, and a marvellous repertory of near extinct Cockney songs, George was very attractive to the opposite sex, and more than one of his fellow students was disposed to fall in love with him. So was I.[20]

So began Barbara Wootton's second marriage, which lasted almost 30 years until George's death in 1964. She still kept the surname from her first marriage. It may have been simply convenience: she was beginning to be well known, but I suspect there was more to this than that. Jack was her first and greatest love. She married George in July 1935 at the Fulham Register Office 'by the only woman registrar in the country'.[21] The marriage began in a blaze of publicity, George being then a taxi driver, albeit that he had been awarded a full-time scholarship at the London School of Economics, and Barbara being a university 'don'. Together they were news.

How satisfactory was this marriage? It is difficult to say. Her biographer Ann Oakley says it was an unlikely union.[22] George came from a working-class family, she from the upper middle class. The real problem was, according to Barbara, that George was a natural polygamist, who from the earliest days of their marriage had always found it necessary to have a secondary wife round the corner.[23] For her part, she says her failings were that she was too much occupied with her own affairs and too reluctant to modify her way of life to make an easy marriage partner.[24] The surprise therefore was that the marriage lasted as long as it did. Yet George and Barbara lived together in what Barbara describes 'as in a civilised way' for 21 of those 30 years. They never divorced. One other life-changing event occurred, or rather it was a life-changing nonevent, for there were no children of the marriage. Barbara said George set his face resolutely against having a child, not wanting to be tied down in any way, although Barbara would greatly have liked to have a family. She said she 'had to realise the price of persistence was too high'.[25] Although she includes this in her Autobiography, she deals with it only briefly, and then only in a small part of one paragraph, but I suspect she felt this deeply. She said of her first marriage that she and Jack had 'wanted to produce a considerable family'.[26] Many years later, she told me how much she regretted not having children.

At the age of 28, in February 1926, Barbara Wootton was appointed a magistrate.[27] This was another first; she was not of course the first woman to be appointed magistrate, but the first to become a magistrate at an age at which as a woman she was ineligible to vote. (At the time, the voting age for women was 30 years, changed to 21 years only in 1928.) This was of course further grist to the Wootton mill; she saw the absurdity of being appointed as able to dispense justice before being considered suitable and mature enough to cast a vote.

She sat on the bench for nearly 50 years, many of those as Chairman, with 20 of those years in the juvenile courts, of which 16 were as Chairman. There is a chapter in her Autobiography, simply called 'Magistrate', where she wrote of the poignancy and humour of the courts and of those offenders appearing before it. Being a magistrate was clearly an important part of Barbara's life, not the least that it provided information on the court system, sentencing practices and the offenders themselves. It was a constant throughout her life. She noted that in those 50 or so years, 'the business of the Courts has changed out of all recognition mainly owing to the invention of the internal combustion engine'. That is to say, traffic offences account for over 60% of court cases, so that every justice's criminal work falls into two classes, motoring and what she called 'ordinary' crime.[28]

During the Second World War, George registered as a conscientious objector, and Barbara, being too old for any women's service, was a vigorous campaigner for a number of causes, especially 'World Government' and a more federalised international order. She still regarded herself as an economist, having published two important books that straddled the war years: *Lament for Economics* in 1938 and *The Social Foundations of Wage Policy*, published 17 years later in 1955. The first takes the economics of the time to task for being of no practical use, being unintelligible to the ordinary man, for being riddled with and weakened by internal disputes to ignore reality, and for being an apologia for capitalism. The second book on wage policy had a more lasting legacy, where she argued for a rational wage policy, not one based on collective bargaining, which she saw as the last stronghold of collective *laissez faire*. Neither book was very well received, the first because it upset traditional economists, and the second because it came at a time when Trade Union (TU) power in Britain was at its height and collective bargaining seen as an expression of that power.

Barbara Wootton's biographer saw this latter book on wage policy as being the end of her period as an economist and the beginning of her transition to sociology. If so, then the transition was neither sharp nor complete; Barbara continued to write and lecture on economics right up to her death. She was after all a Member of the Royal Commission on Civil Service Pay and Conditions in 1953–1955, and in 1975 she accepted an invitation to give a prestigious lecture to LSE on the future of the British economy.[29] In line with her earlier thinking and true to form, the theme of the lecture was that the economy should serve the public interest. Yet slowly she began to move more and more towards a generic social science approach.

The opportunity came when she was offered a Readership in Social Science at Bedford College University of London in 1944. This was converted to a Professorship some two years later. She had applied for a Chair in Sociology at LSE, but this was awarded to T.H. Marshall, a more mainstream sociologist; the Bedford College post therefore was her second choice. As things turned out, the Chair at Bedford led eventually to one of her most important contributions, the book *Social Science and Social Pathology*, published some 15 years later in 1959. In the meantime, the post at Bedford provided her with contact with students and the opportunity to develop her thinking about the social sciences.

At Bedford, she was full of optimism for the future. She saw it as providing opportunities for large-scale social science research. She may not have seen herself as a sociologist, although she was a founder member of the British Sociological Association in 1951, was Chairman in 1957–1959 and President from 1959–1964. And although she published books and articles in criminology, it is doubtful if she saw herself as a criminologist either. She did, however, call herself a social scientist, thinking this generic term more easily fitting to her wider range of interests[30] – or rather not so much a social scientist, but a scientist of social studies.[31]

She had always been indissolubly attached to the writings of Comte, Mill and Spencer, and later to the writings and ideas of Booth and the Webbs. Of these, one can see the most important influence being that of John Stuart Mill. Like Mill, and others such as Comte and the Webbs, she also had faith in a natural science of society. Comte for example believed that the scientific method as applied to the social sciences would produce knowledge, and this would be scientific knowledge about the workings of the social system. Others held a similar belief in the importance of the emergence of social science. All this fitted neatly with Barbara Wootton's own philosophy. She saw herself as in direct lineal descent from Mill *et al.* Her philosophy was positivist in its belief that the realities of the social world can be quantified, and that such an exercise is the key to social progress.[32]

Barbara Wootton's philosophy also followed from Mill for she was first and foremost a Utilitarian. The first question she asked was always, did this or that policy promote happiness? If it did, it was acceptable; if not, then it should be rejected. And there was always a second question: what is the evidence for this or that policy? 'Evidence' was the ever-constant component of Barbara Wootton's thinking. She railed against those whose assertions were not based on evidence. There was one striking example in 1965: the debate in the House of Lords on the bill to abolish the death penalty. A number of speakers claimed an increase in the numbers of murders in countries in which the death penalty was abolished.

> Yet no attempt whatever was made by those who advocated the retention of hanging either to criticise this evidence or to produce further facts that pointed in the contrary direction. One after another speakers were content to say more murders would follow if murderers were no longer hanged.[33]

Such evidence as there was for those supporting the death penalty, said Barbara Wootton 'came, one can only suppose upon introspection into their own sanguinary impulses'.[34] These were straightforward points about the importance of evidence, worth making then, and certainly still worth making again today.

One of Barbara Wootton's most important books, entitled *Testament for Social Science*, was published in 1950 whilst she was at Bedford College. It developed and expanded the methodology developed by positivist thinkers such as Mill. Its subtitle was 'An essay in the application of scientific method to human problems'. As the title and subtitle suggest, the book sets out Barbara Wootton's blueprint for the role of social science and its part in producing answers to the many problems that beset us.[35] It was written in an optimistic time when in spite of the devastation of World War II, there was a common belief that the future was bright, and 'things would be better this time'.

She opens the debate by stating the three stages of the scientific process; first the accurate observation of data, followed by the formulation of a hypothesis, and finally the promotion of the hypothesis by empirical verification of a law. The scientific method, according to Barbara Wootton, is simply the attempt to acquire knowledge of general laws directly or indirectly by experience through the use of our five senses. The problem she had was to determine how far a parallel attempt can be made to acquire knowledge about human relationships.[36] Her conclusion was that there is still a long way to go, but the journey, however difficult and lengthy, will be possible and certainly worth it. The rewards, she believed, would be a reduction in social distress, and a removal of the clouds of superstition under which many still live.

She believed the difference between the natural and social sciences was one of degree, not kind. Objections based on the assertion that humans are born with free will or are predetermined can, she said, be safely bypassed. 'We can predict that there will be crowds in Putney on boat race day without being committed to the doctrine that people are not free to choose whether they will go to see the race or not.'[37] What hold us back, she says, have been two main causes of confusion, a muddled biological analysis based on the assertion that human societies are organisms, and the influence of pseudoscientific systems such as those associated with the name of Marx.[38] The first, she says, was because human societies do not have a life cycle, and societies or civilisations do not 'die'; to state otherwise is to use a picturesque metaphor which opens the door to disastrous fallacies. The second was because the writings of Marx have been translated into a 'system' leading to a search for scriptural authority, and not empirical evidence. 'Keeping in line with what

Stalin says that Lenin said that Marx said is much the same as keeping in line with the Bible.'[39]

Testament for Social Science was not well received in Britain, but was rather more so in the USA, where sociology had a more pronounced tradition. It was not saying anything new; 'sociology as a science' was part of a debate in most if not all undergraduate sociology courses of the late 1950s and early 1960s. What was new in *Testament*, however, was what one reviewer called 'the bright eyed and bushy tailed enthusiasm' of the book itself, or as another called the 'wonderfully clear statement of the nature of scientific thinking'.[40] These qualities, however, were not sufficient to have the intended impact: she mentions the book only once in her Autobiography, although she does refer to the plight of social science and its likely impact. Her conclusion is that social science has had an exponential growth within academic circles, but outside the academic world 'the light of that dawn hardly seems to have penetrated'.[41]

Unfortunately, Barbara Wootton's hopes and expectations surrounding her Chair at Bedford College were also not realised. In her Autobiography, she complains about some of her academic colleagues. It was all about research funds which were allocated and 'earmarked' for Barbara Wootton's social science department but met with objections from colleagues in other departments – so much so that colleagues 'so deeply grudged to our department money which was in no case available for their own that they would prefer that the college should forego these funds altogether rather than that we should have them'.[42] As she says, 'This experience came as a great shock to me', which she put down to 'a compound of hostility, jealousy and ignorance, – in what proportion I should not like to say'.[43] She saw part of the hostility to attitudes in the academic world from those who believed that any word beginning with 'socio' must inevitably end with 'alism', but she could have added it also produced a measure of distrust about social science generally which unhappily still exists. The upshot of all this was that Barbara decided she could no longer remain responsible for a department 'so absurdly hamstrung and which operated in such an absurd environment'.[44] It so happened that at this time the Nuffield Foundation had considered funding a project on the fruitfulness of social research. Barbara Wootton applied, was accepted and was given a five-year Research Fellowship to 'examine the results of research in criminology and allied social science subjects'.

The result was *Social Science and Social Pathology*, published in 1959. It is an extraordinary book, highly influential at the time, but like *Testament for Social Science*, also now largely forgotten. It was, however, well reviewed. *The Times Literary Supplement* called it 'a brilliantly organised survey of contemporary opinion on social pathology', *Education* said 'an enlightened Home Secretary would make it compulsory reading for every Magistrate', and *The New Statesman* said it was 'a sociological study of exceptional interest and distinction'. *The Listener* said Barbara Wootton had performed a major service to social science. It was, however, a product of its time, but it is also a book which contains much that is timeless, especially in terms of that relating to crime and criminological research.

In *Social Science and Social Pathology*, Barbara Wootton sought to discover what social science could say about the nature and extent of social pathology in the then-contemporary Britain. It covers a wide range of pathologies, some of which we would not include nowadays, discusses some questions we would find less interesting and leaves out some we would include. For example, there is a section on 'Illegitimacy' and another on 'Divorce', but nothing of course on 'Substance Abuse', which did not become a problem in Britain until four or five years after publication – all of which unintentionally underlines one of Barbara Wootton's basic points, that social pathology is elusive and difficult to define. In Chapter 9, one of the most famous chapters, there was a blistering attack on social work. Other chapters are equally interesting and relevant, if not always for their content then for their comments on the methodology used by social scientists generally and criminologists in particular. The chapter on 'Twelve criminological hypotheses' is a case in point. It was an analysis of 21 research studies which related to the more popular current hypotheses about the causes or characteristics of crime and delinquency. The conclusion was that although the studies were chosen for their methodological merit, with the requirements that each should meet certain fixed criteria, they produced only meagre results. 'And beyond this we cannot go.'[45] Not a very optimistic conclusion, but one which illustrated how poor most criminological studies were in terms of their method, and how most were 'soaked' in value judgements. A similar conclusion was reached in the chapter on 'Mental disorder', where 'mental health and ill health cannot be defined in objective scientific terms that are free of subjective moral judgements.'[46] (A more detailed examination will be given in Chapter 3.) Unsurprisingly, these conclusions were not well received by the professionals concerned, but have remained the standards by which later research has had to be judged.

Shortly before *Social Science and Social Pathology* was published, Barbara Wootton became a member of the House of Lords, taking the title of Baroness Wootton of Abinger. It was another first. She was not of course the first woman peer, but she was the first woman to be created a peer under the Life Peerages Act, which for the first time admitted non-hereditary peers and women to Britain's upper house. She was aged 61. Interestingly enough, although she was still 'Mrs. Barbara Wright', being still married to George, she took the title Baroness Wootton.[47] Although she was at the age at which many consider retiring, this was for Barbara, and for criminology, the beginning of a very productive period, lasting well into the next two decades. Her publishing output remained prodigious, her Committee membership equally so, and her contribution to Parliamentary debates important, especially concerning penal affairs.

George died in 1964, but they had been apart for many years. George had no wish to divorce, and Barbara said she had not the heart to go through with it.[48] George lived for eight years after their separation, but even before that in their last few years together they did not share a common life. Barbara moved out of the matrimonial home (she said she never forgave herself for deserting him) and moved to High Barn in Dorking Surrey, where she remained until her death in 1988. She describes High Barn as rich in satisfactions, the house, the garden and the neighbourhood giving conscious daily pleasure. She shared the accommodation with companions. Vera Seal was a regular visitor and through the years was Barbara's most loyal and constant companion. Barbara had a deep-seated dislike of personal service, doubtless due to her early years in Cambridge, and assumed the roles of charwoman, secretary, gardener and stable boy. And then there were the donkeys. Barbara describes these as ideal companions, quite capable of looking after themselves, but intelligent, kind and affectionate. One was called 'Miranda', having been born during a tempest.

In spite of the pleasures High Barn must have given, it must also have been a fairly lonely time in spite of the companions who shared her life. Yet it was also a very productive time as far as her work was concerned. From the date of publication of *Social Science and Social Pathology*, it was possible to identify more than 100 published works. In addition, she was a member of numerous committees. These covered a wide range of subjects including criminology. She still published on economics, but wrote also on social policy – her interest in the welfare state was lifelong, and in fact two of her last three publications were entitled 'Reflections on the Welfare State' and 'The Moral Basis of the Welfare State'.[49] In her later years, she also published on 'The Right to Die', and 'Death Whose Right to Choose'. Unsurprisingly, the rate of publications dropped in her last five or six years, her last publications being in 1985, three years before her death.

She was appointed to the BBC Board of Governors in 1950, a date misprinted in *Who's Who* as 1590. Barbara thought it a shame that the mistake was put right in the succeeding issue, because it provided every Chairman who had to introduce her at meetings with a ready-made joke.[50] She had broadcast regularly for a number of years; her earliest broadcasts were in the interwar years. She wrote amusingly about the facilities offered at the BBC, for example how the lunches varied according to the supposed prestige of the audience. At the bottom of the scale came overseas broadcasts, where inferior sandwiches were provided. Next in the hierarchy came *Woman's Hour*, where a better meal was served, 'women being a cut above foreigners but not quite first class citizens'. It was 'only at the level of *Panorama* or the old *Brains Trust* does one attain to the luxury of a really slap-up meal'.[51] There was also the problem of the lavatories for women. There were only two women Governors, the other being Stella Reading. The nailbrush on the toilet was chained to the basin, and the two women wondered which of them was the target of this precaution.[52]

She singled out the Athenaeum Club for particular attention as it was not until 2002, some 15 years after Barbara's death, that women members were admitted. First, she was clearly aggrieved that it remained a 'Gentleman's Club' for male members only, and an important and influential one at that. So, said Barbara, 'We look forward to a far greater distinction than entry into the House of Lords and that is entry for women into the Athenaeum Club.'[53] Then, as a male-only institution, it thwarted her influence over a particular Committee.

> A more important consideration is the fact that if the members do not lunch together they may break up into small separate parties. Years ago I learnt this lesson on one committee a nucleus of those members always slipped out to lunch together at The Athenaeum where of course no women was eligible to join them. During the afternoon session this clique shared a remarkable unanimity of the various issues that came before us.[54]

She never forgave the Athenaeum for offering sanctuary to male club members, in so doing giving them a particular advantage.

In her Autobiography, Barbara noted how there were significant changes to broadcasting over the years, most notably in the way it had surrendered to what she called the standards of show business and journalism. That is to say, presentation had become more important than content, with the programme producers assuming more and more importance. She noted too the contrast with book-reviewing and thought that serious book reviewers would be 'greatly surprised if it became the practice for their works to be judged solely on grounds of style'.[55] She added, 'Under its charter the BBC is required to provide information, education and entertainment: but these are or should be three distinct functions, nor is there any justification for the first and second being subsumed under the third.'[56]

Her first major appointment as far as criminology is concerned was to the Probation Advisory Committee. This was as far back as 1946. Then there was her appointment to the Streatfeild Committee on the Business of the Criminal Courts in England and Wales. It was set up in June 1958 and reported in 1961. It recommendations led directly to the Criminal Justice Act in 1962. There were nine members of the Committee. Its main recommendations were straightforward and not contentious, simply that a greater number of cases could be tried in the magistrates' courts and that trial waiting periods could be shortened by requiring the then Quarter Sessions to sit more often.

This was followed in 1964 by Barbara Wootton's appointment to the Royal Commission on the Penal System. This was not the first Royal Commission to fall short in terms of expectations or results, nor the last, but fall short it did. She said little about it in her Autobiography except to say that Commissions should not consist of more than a dozen or so persons, and membership must be drawn from persons who have already at least a working knowledge of the matters with which they are concerned. She thought 'the issues of today are too complex and too pressing to wait while laymen learn their way about worlds to which they come as complete strangers.'[57] Were these perhaps comments on that Royal Commission which altogether had 16 members, comprising Barbara Wootton and Professor Leon Radzinowicz, a professor of criminology, plus

> a trade unionist who had no contact with the system of justice, seven JPs two of whom were also MPs one being a fervent advocate of capital punishment, an English and a Scottish judge, a psychiatrist with much experience of offenders, a Professor of Social Medicine, a Bishop, and a Secretary of a County Council all under the Chairmanship of a former Chancellor of the Exchequer who had no close acquaintance with penal matters.[58]

The terms of reference were astonishingly wide, including 'to re-examine the concepts and purposes that underlie the punishment and treatment of offenders and decide how they are realised'. Apparently all the Commissioners did was argue, making and remaking plans for the future, hearing 'platitudinous evidence' and 'debating the niceties of penal philosophies'. Eventually the Commission was disbanded, being replaced in 1966 with a permanent Advisory Council on the Penal System, which had more restricted terms of reference and was much more likely to produce effective policies. Barbara Wootton was a member of that Advisory Council. It is not of course possible to say how and in what ways she influenced its reports, but some influence she certainly had. She was no shrinking violet when it came to putting forth her views.

In the period following the Royal Commission, that is between 1968 and 1970, there were two influential Government Reports, both largely due to Barbara Wootton. The first in 1968, entitled 'Cannabis', was a Report by the Advisory Committee on Drug Dependence. Or more technically, it was a report by the Hallucinogens Sub-Committee, as Lysergic Acid Diethylamide (LSD) was included. It was always called the 'Wootton Report' as it was completed largely under Barbara Wootton's influence. This subcommittee was asked 'to review available evidence on the pharmacological, clinical, pathological, social and legal aspects of these drugs'. It reported at a time when the drug problem was beginning to be seen as reaching epidemic proportions, and with the courts being faced with a new type of offender. It would have been easy and popular to have produced a report which surrendered to the growing hysteria, but the 'Cannabis' report did otherwise. It offered a view which was a sober account of the dangers, and gave a realistic view of the links with the use of other drugs. As such it pleased few, offended many, and initially was largely ignored.

The second Report had a different outcome. This Report of the Advisory Council on the Penal System was entitled 'Non Custodial and Semi Custodial Penalties'. In November 1966, the Home Secretary asked the Advisory Council on the Penal System to 'consider what changes and additions might be made in the existing range of non custodial penalties disabilities and other requirements which may be imposed on offenders'. The Council again appointed a subcommittee under the chairmanship of Lady Wootton. The outcome was the introduction of the Community Service Order, another of Barbara Wootton's bright ideas, and one of which she was also justifiably proud.

Taken together, these two Reports cemented Barbara Wootton's reputation within the world of criminal justice and public policy. She said later that an office within the Home Office was where she spent most of her time, and one can see why this was so. Yet before and after these

Reports, i.e., in 1963 and 1978, Barbara Wootton published two important books: the the Hamlyn Lectures entitled *Crime and the Criminal Law* and the other *Crime and Penal Policy*. The Hamlyn Lectures were another first; this time Barbara Wootton was the first layman rather than a lawyer to give the lectures. She said she offered them as 'the product of dual experience extending over more than 30 years, – experience as a Magistrate and as a professional social scientist'.[59] They were well received. She also wrote a number of papers and gave numerous public lectures; it was indeed a busy period. And of course she was also active in the House of Lords. She spoke in numerous debates. She was indeed a very public figure.

There were numerous public honours and foreign speaking tours during this period. She was given 13 honorary degrees from both sides of the Atlantic, including one from Columbia University. Yet the one that gave her the greatest pleasure was from the University of Cambridge, this giving her a 'special delight'. Her biographer says 'The degree less Mrs. Wootton who had endured the insult of having to lecture under a male name in Cambridge in 1921 now seemed to have passed beyond the stage of notoriety to a level of widespread recognition.'[60] She was also made a Companion of Honour in 1977, a rare and exceptional award given only to those who have made 'outstanding achievements in the arts, music, politics, industry or religion'. And in spite of her criticisms of psychiatry, she was also made an Honorary Fellow of the Royal College of Psychiatrists in 1979 as well as delivering the prestigious Maudsley lecture. Also, there were foreign lecture tours, including to Australia and Japan, where she was again honoured.

Barbara was a lifelong supporter of the Labour Party and a persistent critic of a society which is hierarchical in structure and produces such disparities in wealth and opportunity. Chapter 2 of *Social Science and Social Pathology* is entitled 'Social pathology and the social hierarchy', where she sets out the links with poverty and crime. She notes in the opening paragraph how in a hierarchical society it is natural to expect that the distribution of socially unacceptable behaviour to conform to, or at least be shaped by, the pattern of hierarchy. She also notes how the prevalence of criminality in the lower classes is easily demonstrated by the use of definitions which automatically exclude crimes to which the upper classes are most likely to be addicted. The chapter itself is a sympathetic attempt to represent the plight of those at the bottom, although Barbara herself knew little of poverty or deprivation – she was born in Cambridge, worked mostly in London (including Regents Park) and moved to Dorking in Surrey.

Although she was a member of the Labour Party and there were numerous invitations to enter politics as a Labour Party MP, Barbara always refused. She was right to do so. She was, I think, ill suited to be a Party politician voting according to the demands of the Party Whips. She sat as a Cross Bencher in the House of Lords, able to vote according to her assessment of the policies presented. This was her strength and was well within her disposition. She was an iconoclast, rather than a member of a group or Party, always wanting to advance her particular cause. She would have seen the demands of Party politics as wanting to confine and restrict her, and that would never do.

The last 25 years or so of her life, mainly at High Barn, were such that Barbara continued to work, sit in the House of Lords, and for the first decade or so travelled widely, giving invitation lectures. Yet her health began to deteriorate, and in her mid-80s she said she had had 'enough of life'. Towards the end, she cut a rather lonely figure, looked after mainly by her lifelong friend Vera Seal. Vera was devoted to her and incidentally was mainly responsible for the production of the four volumes of Barbara's writing produced shortly after her death. One of the problems was that Barbara's personal relations were never easy; she was often prickly and was a difficult person with which to have an easy rapport – although it was said her students adored her. A colleague at Bedford College said, 'It was partly I think because if she thought you weren't talking sense she found it difficult not to convey that.'[61] Barbara once complained about a certain professor having poor social relations. That was rich coming from Barbara.

In her final years, she became alarmingly suspicious and accusatory, even towards her closest friends. A one point, she accused Vera Seal of stealing her wedding ring. There was another incident where she accused her favourite chauffeur of wanting to harm her. At the ceremony at which she was presented with copies of the *Festschrift*, she seemed to know she was the central figure, but whether she knew the implications or meaning of what was happening is difficult to say. There was a deeply ironic moment at that presentation when the local senior police officer heard about the incident with the chauffeur. He said she should be seen by a social worker under the Mental Health Act!

She summed up her life in her Autobiography saying that for more than 40 years she had the essential foundation of stable happiness: a congenial companion at home with whom to share the day's events (presumably this meant being with George most of the time, as she was writing this in 1967). She often spoke of the importance of having someone with whom to share the day's events, someone to discuss, converse or even perhaps gossip about trifling matters. She saw the deepest satisfactions, however, coming from personal relationships, but she was grateful that nature had endowed her with an active mind, 'the exercise of which has from the days of my adolescence been both a continual source of enjoyment and a constant comfort in adversity'.[62] She said she has 'enjoyed recognition and success' and then added somewhat precipitously that she had 'lived to see much of what I have striven for actually come to pass'.[63] One can see why she might have seen things this way; but she might have been a little too optimistic.

She died on 11 July 1988. There was a short, nonreligious funeral at Golders Green Crematorium in London. For reasons which are not altogether clear, there was no subsequent memorial service. And for other reasons, also not altogether clear, there were few mourners at her funeral. It was a strange affair; one would have expected countless representatives from the numerous bodies, official and otherwise, of which she had been a member: the House of Lords, the BBC, the British Sociological Association, etc., but there were few peers (Lord Longford came on his bicycle) and only a small group of friends and neighbours. There were also few family members, Vera Seal being the chief mourner. As one of the carers from the nursing home said, 'For a life like that that seemed incredible. This isn't right. This isn't good enough; this wasn't what should have happened.'[64] There were, however, numerous obituaries fulsome in their praise of someone whose life was devoted to public service and who seemed to have achieved so much. There were plans for a 'Barbara Wootton Chair in Social Research', but like the memorial service, nothing happened.

At the end of *Testament for Social Science*, Barbara Wootton quoted approvingly from Leonard Woolf, who considered that the sordid and savage story of history has been written by man's irrationality, and the thin precarious crust of civilisation, which has from time to time been built over this bloody mess, has always been built by reason. Barbara Wootton's hope and expectation for the future was that there would be less of that 'bloody mess', were the principles of social science to be more universally applied. That is to say, and at a more specific level, she would expect that a positivist Utilitarian approach to criminology would reduce crime, and a similar approach would produce a more rational policy of criminal justice. I doubt if her hopes could ever be realised, for she seemed not to include the whims of politicians and the reluctance to introduce or produce an evidence-based policy – or of the ambitions of some criminologists to avoid such endeavours. Nonetheless, she kept trying, and would presumably urge us to do likewise.

She may have been 'A Critical Woman' according to her biographer, Ann Oakley, but she was also a concerned one, and a supremely successful one at that.

Notes

1 There were four Royal Commissions of which she was a member. They are: Workmen's Compensation, appointed 1938; the Press, appointed 1947; Civil Service, appointed 1954; and the Penal System, appointed 1964. She was also a member of four Departmental Committees: the Colwyn Committee on National Debt and Taxation (she wrote every word of the Minority Report); on Shop Hours, appointed 1946; the Streatfeild Committee on Business of the Criminal Courts, appointed 1958; and on Criminal Statistics, appointed 1963. She was also a Member of the Advisory Committee on Drug Dependence, and was Chairman of the Hallucinogens Sub Committee Report on Cannabis in 1968.

2 Aldridge M (1986) An organising female with a brief case. In Bean PT and Whynes D (eds) *Barbara Wootton Social Science and Public Policy. Essays in her Honour*. Tavistock p. 41.

3 This was a comment from a distinguished law professor, John Smith See. Smith J (1986) Responsibility in criminal law. In Bean PT and Whynes D (eds) *Barbara Wootton Social Science and Public Policy. Essays in her Honour*. Tavistock pp. 141–155.

4 See Aldridge M (1986) An organising female with a brief case. In Bean PT and Whynes D (eds) *Barbara Wootton Social Science and Public Policy. Essays in her Honour*. Tavistock. op. cit. pp. 1–16.

5 Oakley A (2011) *A Critical Woman*. Bloomsbury Academic p. 295.

6 Wootton B (1967) *In a World I Never Made*. George Allen and Unwin p. 9.

7 Ibid. p. 46.

8 Ibid. p. 50.

9 In a conversation I had with Barbara nearly 20 years later, she still said she was unable to pass the Rubens Hotel without feeling a surge of emotion.

10 Wootton B (1967) *In a World I Never Made*. George Allen and Unwin. op. cit. p. 52.

11 Ibid. p. 54.

12 Ibid. p. 59.

13 Ibid. p. 60.

14 Aldridge M (1986) An organising female with a briefcase. In Bean PT and Whynes D (eds) *Barbara Wootton. Social Science and Public Policy. Essays in her Honour*. Tavistock. op. cit. p. 40.

15 Wootton B (1967) *In a World I Never Made*. George Allen and Unwin. op. cit. p. 270.

16 Ibid. p. 160.

17 Ibid. p. 147.

18 Oakley A (2011) *A Critical Woman*. Bloomsbury Academic p. 128.

19 Ibid. p. 101.

20 Wootton B (1967) *In a World I Never Made*. George Allen and Unwin. op. cit. p. 85.

21 Ibid. pp. 86–87.
22 Oakley A (2011) A *Critical Woman*. Bloomsbury Academic. op. cit. p. 124.
23 Ibid. p. 138.
24 Ibid.
25 Ibid.
26 Ibid. p. 49.
27 It was in her capacity as a magistrate at Bow Street Magistrates' Court that I first saw her. And a formidable presence she was.
28 Wootton B (1967) *In a World I Never Made*. George Allen and Unwin. op. cit. p. 219.
29 Oakley A (2011) A *Critical Woman*. Bloomsbury Academic. op. cit. p. 181.
30 See McGregor Lord (1986) Champion of the impossible. In Bean PT and Whynes D (eds) *Barbara Wootton Social Science and Public Policy. Essays in her Honour*. Tavistock pp. 1–16 for an account of how she selected 'Social Studies' in preference to sociology and McGregor Lord (1986) Champion of the impossible. In Bean PT and Whynes D (eds) *Barbara Wootton Social Science and Public Policy. Essays in her Honour*. Tavistock. op. cit. p. 9.
31 Oakley A (2011) A *Critical Woman*. Bloomsbury Academic. op. cit. p. 114.
32 Ibid. p. 188.
33 Wootton B (1967) *In a World I Never Made*. George Allen and Unwin. op. cit. p. 214.
34 Ibid. pp. 215–216.
35 Wootton B (1950) *Testament for Social Science*. George Allen and Unwin.
36 Ibid. p. 6.
37 Ibid. p. 179.
38 Ibid. p. 72.
39 Ibid. p. 86.
40 Oakley A (2011) A *Critical Woman*. Bloomsbury Academic. op. cit. pp. 198–199.
41 Wootton B (1967) *In a World I Never Made*. George Allen and Unwin. op. cit. p. 213.
42 Ibid. p. 103.
43 Ibid.
44 Ibid. p. 104.
45 Wootton B (1959) *Social Science and Social Pathology*. George Allen and Unwin p. 135.
46 Ibid. p. 226.
47 At the inauguration ceremony, Barbara refused to swear on the Bible as part of her oath of allegiance. This created a delay. Two old Tories on the bench opposite wondered out loud what accounted for the holdup. 'She doesn't believe in God', said one. 'Why the Devil not?' said the other. Oakley A (2011) A *Critical Woman*. Bloomsbury Academic. op. cit. p. 19.
48 Wootton B (1967) *In a World I Never Made*. George Allen and Unwin. op. cit. p. 139.
49 Bean PT and MacPherson S (eds) (1983) *Approaches to Welfare*. Routledge pp. 282–293 and Bean PT, Ferris J and Whynes D (eds) (1985) *In Defence of Welfare*. Tavistock pp. 31–45.
50 Wootton B (1967) *In a World I Never Made*. George Allen and Unwin. op. cit. p. 258.
51 Ibid. pp. 259–260.

52 Oakley A (2011) A *Critical Woman*. Bloomsbury Academic. op. cit. p. 18.
53 Ibid. p. 19.
54 Wootton B (1967) *In a World I Never Made*. George Allen and Unwin. op. cit. pp. 251–252.
55 Ibid. p. 265.
56 Ibid.
57 Oakley A (2011) A *Critical Woman*. Bloomsbury Academic. op. cit. p. 257.
58 Ibid.
59 Wootton B (1963) *Crime and the Criminal Law: Reflections of a Magistrate and a Social Scientist*. (The Hamlyn Lectures) Stevens and Sons. (Second Edition 1981 with postscripts to each chapter) p. 1.
60 Oakley A (2011) A *Critical Woman*. Bloomsbury Academic. op. cit. p. 300.
61 Ibid. p. 193.
62 Wootton B (1967) *In a World I Never Made*. George Allen and Unwin. op. cit. p. 143.
63 Ibid.
64 Oakley A (2011) A *Critical Woman*. Bloomsbury Academic. op. cit. p. 343.

References for publications by Barbara Wootton

A more complete list of Barbara Wootton's publications can be found in Seal V and Bean P.T. (1992) (eds) *Barbara Wootton. Selected Writings*. MacMillan Vols 1–4.

Wootton B (1950) *Testament for Social Science*. George Allen and Unwin.

Wootton B (1959) *Social Science and Social Pathology*. George Allen and Unwin.

Wootton B (1962) A *Social Scientists Approach to Maternal Deprivation in Deprivation of Maternal Care; A Reassessment of Its Effects*. WHO pp. 63–73.

Wootton B (1963) *Crime and the Criminal Law: Reflections of a Magistrate and a Social Scientist*. (The Hamlyn Lectures) Stevens and Sons. (Second Edition 1981 with postscripts to each chapter).

Wootton B (1967) *In a World I Never Made. Autobiographical Reflections*. George Allen and Unwin.

Wootton B (1972) Crime responsibility and prevention. Reprinted In Gerber R and McAnany D (eds) *Contemporary Punishment*. University of Notre Dame Press pp. 164–175.

Wootton B (1978) *Crime and Penal Policy; Reflections on Fifty Years Experience*. Allen and Unwin.

Wootton B (1992) The administration of justice. Lecture given to the University of Leeds. Reprinted In Seal V and Bean P (eds) *Barbara Wootton Selected Writings Vol. 1 Crime and the Penal System* pp. 95–108.

Wootton B. (1992) Some reflections on the first five years of community service. Reprinted In Seal V and Bean P (eds) *Barbara Wootton Selected Writings Vol. 1 Crime and the Penal System* pp. 143–145.

Wootton B (1992) Who are the criminals? Reprinted In Seal V and Bean P (eds) *Barbara Wootton Selected Writings Vol. 1 Crime and the Penal System* pp. 109–117.

Wootton B (1992) Time and the drug scene. Reprinted In Seal V and Bean P (eds) *Barbara Wootton Selected Writings Vol. 1 Crime and the Penal System* pp. 135–137.

Wootton B (1992) Sickness or sin? Reprinted In Seal V and Bean P (eds) *Barbara Wootton Selected Writings Vol. 2 Crime and the Penal System* pp 76–84.

Wootton B (1992) The law, the doctor and the deviant. Reprinted In Seal V and Bean P (eds) *Barbara Wootton Selected Writings Vol. 2 Crime and the Penal System* pp. 61–75.

Wootton B (1992) Psychiatry Ethics and the law. Reprinted In Seal V and Bean P (eds) *Barbara Wootton Selected Writings Vol. 2 Crime and the Penal System* pp. 1–12.

Chapter 2

Social pathology, the courts and the penal system

Barbara Wootton's range of interests were sufficiently wide to make it difficult to put them into neat, self-contained packages. What I have included in this chapter overlaps with that which follows. For example, the *Report on Non Custodial Penalties* has been placed in Chapter 3, but could have easily been included here.

To some extent, this is a hybrid chapter including a number of different features loosely connected under a heading of 'Social pathology, the courts and the penal system'. In the first part, I want to look at what Barbara Wootton defined as social pathology, which includes the so-called Bowlby thesis, problem families and 'Twelve criminological hypotheses'. Then I want to look at the courts. Barbara Wootton was a magistrate for many years and throughout retained an interest in the courts and court procedures. This is followed by discussions on sentencing, the tariff and juvenile justice. She sat for many years in the juvenile courts and held interesting views on the way the juvenile justice system should develop. Then there is a discussion on Barbara Wootton's views on the penal system, ending with her contributions to some of the House of Lords debates concentrating mainly on the Second Reading of the Murder (Abolition of the Death Penalty) Bill.

Social pathology, selected features

In 1959 when *Social Science and Social Pathology* was published, Barbara Wootton was 62 years of age. She said in her Autobiography this would be her last book – it wasn't; she published the Hamlyn Lectures entitled *Crime and the Criminal Law* in 1963 and in 1978 *Crime and Penal Policy*. She also published a number of papers and gave numerous public lectures on crime, criminal justice and social pathology. She said that producing *Social Science and Social Pathology* had been extremely exacting as well as extremely interesting, and added 'if I may be forgiven, I am rather proud of it'[1] – and justifiably so. It was a very impressive text. The reviews were, generally speaking, complimentary, even if the book itself was to offend many, especially those in professions such as social work and psychiatry. Essentially, the book was a treatise on methodology, which was not what Barbara Wootton originally intended, but that was how it finally appeared.[2] It covered a wide area.

There are a number of chapters in *Social Science and Social Pathology* which require detailed consideration, two of which I have selected for a brief examination. They might seem outdated nowadays, but I suggest they illustrate much about the clarity of Barbara Wootton's approach. A third chapter entitled 'Twelve criminological hypotheses' is a classic of its kind and is of much greater relevance. Others such as 'Social pathology and the concepts of "Mental Health and Mental Illness"', and another, 'Mental disorder and the problem of moral and criminal responsibility', are dealt with in later chapters of this volume.

The term 'social pathology' is rarely used nowadays, although it was commonplace in the 1950s. Barbara Wootton defined it 'as antisocial behaviour, or ways of behaving that are socially troublesome'. This obviously included criminal behaviour but also includes behaviour which violates generally accepted standards. It is not a satisfactory definition, as Barbara Wootton herself recognised. She also recognised that terms like 'nonconformity' are culture-bound, involving additional problems such as locating the point at which 'nonconformity' ranks as 'pathological'. She recognised too that social pathology was influenced by fashion, in the sense that there were certain areas of interest which dominate at certain periods and receive attention out of all proportion to their place in the scheme of things. She called these 'changeable currents of social and political opinion', and recognised that she too was not free of them.[3] Accordingly, the space and attention she gave to certain topics in her definition of social pathology were, she said, not always a measure of their true importance; it was more about their strength and appeal to contemporary social investigators or current public opinion.

With this in mind, what Barbara Wootton included as social pathologies in the 1950s is likely to differ from more modern definitions. She included divorces, illegitimacy and what she called 'other domestic casualties' alongside prostitution and intemperance, as well as 'those persons who have no settled way of life'. She recognised that social norms become increasingly elusive in cultures where there are wide freedoms. In such cultures, social norms become close to being whatever people find happens to please them.

The Bowlby thesis

One particularly cherished and fashionable theory of social pathology popular at the time (i.e., in the mid- to late 1950s) was the so-called Bowlby thesis. Barbara Wootton devoted a chapter to this, although the original study, entitled *Forty Four Juvenile Thieves*,[4] was not included in her list of important studies on 'Twelve criminological hypotheses', discussed later, as the sample size was too small. John Bowlby's most influential study was entitled *Maternal Care and Mental Health* and was prepared initially in 1951 for the World Health Organisation. Its main conclusion was that a child needs to have a 'warm intimate and continuous relationship with his mother, or permanent mother substitute, in which both find satisfaction and enjoyment'. The ill effects of the lack of this experience are said to vary with the degree of separation, but its complete absence was said to have far-reaching effects on character development, and may entirely cripple the child's capacity to make relationships. It may well lead to delinquency.

Bowlby argued on the basis of varied evidence that there was a very strong case for believing that prolonged separation of a child from his mother or mother substitute during the first five years of life stands foremost among the causes of delinquent character development and persistent misbehaviour. He restated the position constantly. Bowlby also claimed that his research showed that maternal separation and parental rejection account for a majority of the more intractable personality defects.

This theory was popular, plausible and influential. Much research was devoted to it, with various researchers in psychiatry and elsewhere busily assessing its impact. Bowlby became an international and influential figure. His theory neatly fitted the spirit of the times, especially a psychoanalytic view of the importance of the way a person's subsequent character was shaped, almost determined, by these early experiences. Also, it came soon after World War II, when the effects and impact of the war, with the attendant absence of fathers, was also being assessed.

Barbara Wootton set about this with gusto. It was the perfect situation for a Woottonesque critique, and she clearly enjoyed it. She saw the theory as being littered with looseness of language, overstated claims and a weak methodology. She thought also that there were hints within the thesis that it was all the woman's fault, and that it was a way of restating an older adage that 'a woman's place was in the home'. She began by saying the theory itself was sometimes expressed in remarkably sweeping terms, so that it embraces a number of quite different hypotheses, many of which point to mutually different conclusions. There were shifting positions, such as saying there were different forms of deprivation – i.e., separation from mother, rejection by mother and loss of mother's affection – terms which appeared to be used interchangeably. Or, saying that deprivation *may* have a deleterious effect, and then being more dogmatic, saying that it *does*. She also objected to claims that maternal deprivation produced results that were irreversible, saying there was hardly any evidence to support this far-reaching conclusion, and there can be no justification for such claims, unless and until the victims of maternal deprivation have been followed right through life.[5]

Her criticisms of the methodology were equally forceful, saying that little consideration was given to the institutions in which some of the children were detained. How did they arrive there? What type and quality of care did they receive within those institutions? 'Nor has adequate information been produced about the reasons which led to the children being uprooted from their homes or about the conditions in which they had lived before this happened.'[6]

Her conclusion was that it is difficult to see why it should have been thought necessary to employ so much costly research with so pretentious a scientific façade in order to demonstrate such homely truths that children need to be dependably loved, and without such love are likely to become frightened, unhappy or retarded – or that children have a better chance of finding dependable love in families than in institutions.[7] Her final assessment? She thought that were there to be any value in the research, then it was chiefly for its exposure of the poor quality of care in most institutions, including hospitals, rather than any claims as to producing a certain type of antisocial personality. These achievements, she said, were social rather than psychological. That the damage was said to be lifelong or irreversible, that maternal deprivation was a major factor in criminal behaviour, or that the younger the child the greater the risk – all these must be regarded as quite unproven hypotheses.[8] She wrote a follow-up report for the WHO, published in 1962, which largely repeated what she had said previously.[9]

This was a typical Wootton-type critique, full of attacks on what she regarded as pretentious claims and sloppy language. The Bowlby thesis fell into disrepute in the 1960s, but how much this was due to Barbara Wootton is difficult to say. Her criticisms must have had some impact. Her view that the institutions themselves require attention would, we would now think, be another 'homely truth', yet at the time was not fully appreciated. She was correct, therefore, in saying that children's backwardness may be due to that failure rather than any other.

The problem family

In a similar vein, Barbara Wootton examined the so-called problem family. This was another of those flavours of the 1950s and 1960s preoccupying many policy makers. The term is no longer used, although it is recognised that a small number of offenders in certain geographical areas commit a disproportionate number of offences and are often steeped and overwhelmed in other problems. At the time, a 'problem family' was, as the name suggests, a family with multiple problems, or in Barbara Wootton's terms, a family with a number of the symptoms of social pathology, invariably lying at the bottom of the socioeconomic scale. It was of earlier interest to the Eugenics Society, who saw this group as producing large numbers of children and multiple forms of inadequacy with an unusual high proportion of mental defectives. With the loss of interest in eugenics, the term 'problem family' became the new subject of interest, promoting much research into 'that lowest stratum of the population which is such a headache to our social reformers'.[10]

Barbara Wootton assessed this research and asked (again) how much was it of practical value. She concluded (again) not very much. She saw also how the criteria changed with the researchers; at one point it was 'dependence on public funds', then at another it was 'the physical squalor of the home'. Later it was defined as 'defective personal relationships often accompanied by mental ill health'. She noted too that the definitions varied according to selected features of the families. In one it was the squalor and the disregard of elementary rules of hygiene, in another it was failure to pay the rent, and in a third it was where the children were neglected. She thought the only common trait was that the family had more than one problem, perhaps also that all had financial problems, but as she pointed out, so did many non-problem families. Other than that, no standard pattern existed. (She thought a 'problem family' could best be defined according to the number of social workers in attendance. Any family with more than three probably fell into this category!) Moreover, she noted how the syndromes identified appeared to reflect the subjective interests of the investigators. That which constituted a 'problem' was almost always defined according to the professional orientation of the researcher – mental disorder by the Medical Officer of Health, squalor by Moral Welfare, and child neglect by the NSPCC – all of which made it difficult to decide on an objective definition of a 'problem family'.

She said there were two additional traps for unwary researchers in which so much of this type of research fell and still remains. First, there is the way in which explanations of poverty were couched in the assumption that the quality of the poor was said to explain their poverty. It was, said Barbara Wootton, part of the problem that much research into problem families failed to distinguish between personal inadequacy and simple economic misfortune.

Then there were the definitions themselves which were simply tautological.

> Thus we reach the near tautological conclusion (in research on problem families) that the proof of the psychopathic personality or emotional immaturity of a problem family is to be found in part at least in the characteristic behaviour which merits its inclusion in this class. Yet none of these labels . . . can have any meaning except in terms of criteria which are themselves independent of the behaviour which they are invoked to explain.[11]

Taken together, Barbara Wootton was clearly unimpressed by the quality of the Bowlby research, or in a later and more refined version, into 'broken homes, and the research into problem families'. She thought many researchers were unable to move beyond the basic problems of definition, or to be clear about the nature of their subject matter. Unless or until these basic problems can be resolved, she thought there was no future for such research or the theories that accompany them. That does not mean their popularity will diminish. She said in another context that theories of a general nature including those such as 'blame it on the parents' will remain popular if only because their generality makes them impossible to disprove.[12]

'Twelve criminological hypotheses'

What of the offenders themselves? What did we know about them? Chapter 3 of *Social Science and Social Pathology*, entitled 'Twelve criminological hypotheses: evidence from twenty one studies', sets the scene. Wootton wanted to examine the evidence relating to some of the more current hypotheses about the causes or the characteristic features of delinquency. Twenty-one studies were selected in accordance with the requirements that each should deal with at least 200 subjects, should contain data on not less than half or nearly half the hypotheses under review, and should be sufficiently substantial to include accounts both of the findings and of the methods used. (Hence the Bowlby thesis was not included, presumably failing one or more of the requirements. It certainly did not have 200 subjects.) In the end, 11 British, 9 American and 1 Swedish study were selected.

The hypotheses selected very much reflected the cultural interests of the time. For example, we would think little nowadays of the importance of club membership, church attendance, family size or mother's employment outside the home. Yet these were 4 of the 12 selected hypotheses. There were others of slightly more current interest such as the broken-home theory (again), and the physical health of the offender. The remaining six are more relevant in today's world; they are the presence of other criminals in the family, the offenders' employment record, the social status or social class of the offender group, poverty of the offenders and truancy from school, together with the educational attainment of the offender.

Barbara Wootton went about these studies with the same rapier-type approach as with the Bowlby thesis and problem families, described by David Downes as both an exhilarating and dismaying experience.[13]

> It displayed a sense of exhilaration because it conveyed a sense of urgency, a biting scorn for waffle, and a clear sense of direction. It dismayed because it laid bare the general poverty of criminology, showing it to be a set of rusting clichés and sloppy generalisations.

Of those six most relevant hypotheses the results are thus:

Other criminals in the family. The general conclusion was that not infrequently other members of the delinquent's family have been in trouble with the law. A major difficulty with these studies was the vagaries of definitions; one author talks of offending mothers, another of fathers and siblings, a third is content with such categories as offending relatives or any offenders in the family. Then there is a lack of comparisons. Some studies include nondelinquents in the family; others not.

Offender's employment record. The general conclusion was that where offenders were of an age to be employed, they were most likely to be classified as 'poor' rather than 'good' workers.

Social status or social class. The general conclusion was that most come from the lower social class. The problem however was that whilst there was an overrepresentation from the lower classes, the extent of this was unknown given that it was not clear to what extent this preponderance exceeds those from the noncriminal equivalent.

Poverty. The general conclusion was that the evidence as to the extent to which offenders can be described as exceptionally poor is conflicting. Whilst many delinquents come from very poor families, many others do not, and anyway much delinquency occurs in relatively well-off families.

Truancy from school. The general conclusion was that offenders are quite likely to have truanted from school. Truants are more than average likely to be delinquents, but the great majority of delinquents are not truants.

Educational attainment. The general conclusion is that many delinquents will have earned poor reputations at school, although their reports may well be prejudiced by their teachers' knowledge of their delinquencies. Delinquent children are likely to be unpopular with their teachers and it was not clear from the studies whether the assessments were made without that knowledge.

Barbara Wootton's conclusions were that the results overall were strikingly negative, in that they hardly proved or disproved any of the current theories. 'They produced only the most meagre and dubiously supported generalisations.' Yet she thought the exercise has not been altogether unprofitable. She said it induced a wholesale scepticism and showed up many technical weaknesses in the field. She said, 'Concentrated attention on technical improvement can be a constructive operation.'[14]

In the chapter entitled 'Conclusions – methodological', many of the problems and failings of that research are reworked, albeit under slightly different headings. There is a further damning critique of the Bowlby thesis, saying again that much time and money was wasted in order to say that the unloved were liable to react against being unloved, a point well known before the research, and likely to remain well known after it was undertaken. Then there were criticisms of the 'Twelve criminological hypotheses', especially of the formulation of the hypotheses where they were framed in loose or general terms. It was here that she noted that theories which last the longest are those which deal in relatively vague categories such as 'bad parents' or 'broken home'. In contrast, more concrete, measurable factors which can more easily be put to the test seem to lose their significance when subject to vigorous scrutiny. And as for 'broken homes', there is still no agreement as to its definition – some researchers include broken by death, divorce or separation, others by desertion, or by long absences on account of illness. One researcher included a parent being 'unemployable', or similarly for truancy. Sometimes this was defined as 'persistent' without any quantitative measurement of what is meant by the term.

There were also further criticisms of the tautological nature of some popular labels, 'where labels masquerade as explanations and tautologies as meaningful statements'.[15] In some of the most quoted research of the time, that of Sheldon and Eleanor Glueck in their study *Unravelling Juvenile Delinquency*, they distinguished the delinquent from the non-delinquent on the basis that delinquents were more neurotic. Barbara Wootton saw that their definition of 'neurotic' meant those who suffer from a feeling of anxiety, a sense of failure or of insecurity, and that these criteria served as the detection of neurotics in the population, delinquent or otherwise. That, she said, was another way of saying neurotics exhibit the symptoms of neurotics, or simply, that neurotics are neurotic. The same with 'psychopathy'. If a persistently antisocial person behaves as he does because he is a psychopath, when psychopathy is defined as being persistently antisocial, then this is the same as saying what puts people to sleep is what puts people to sleep, or that the room is cold because the temperature is low.[16]

There were hints too of the influence of fashion and prejudices of the times (i.e., of the late 1950s), affecting the direction of future research. The emphasis of research on individual offenders, she suggests, reflects the spirit of the times, notably the impact of psychiatry on contemporary thinking. It was indeed extraordinary how psychiatric thinking, or more particularly, how psychoanalytic thinking pervaded much of the criminological thinking in that period. She was correct to see the solution to all social problems, crime in particular, was being personalised, often seen in terms of repairing failed relationships, which of course were best repaired through psychiatric treatment, i.e., talk. This led to a certain kind of criminological research, said Barbara Wootton. She said it was mainly directed towards an understanding of the psychology of offenders rather than being framed in sociological terms. The result, she said, was a picture painted of the typical delinquent provided through unduly narrow limits. That typical delinquent was described thus: being of a particular age, coming from a particular kind of home, living in a particular locality, and eventually having a particular kind of job. Some were neurotic and others needed psychiatric attention, but apart from these nothing much else seemed to happen to them. They were described in terms of 'a framework of a life rather than life itself'.[17]

Have things improved? Have criminologists ironed out the weaknesses identified? Have they gone beyond 'that framework of a life' and described 'that life itself'? In terms of later theories, David Downes thought not much had changed. The weaknesses were still there. In Barbara Wootton's *Festschrift*, he selected another 12 criminological hypotheses, or rather 12 criminological theories (some metatheories), and whilst not able to replicate Barbara Wootton's work, aimed to cull from those theories 'the most pertinent form of evidence or argument against which to evaluate them'.[18] The theories selected included anomie, subcultural theory, differential association, labelling theory and social control theory.

David Downes's conclusion was that of the theories reviewed, he suspected Barbara Wootton would give approval to social control theory, this being relatively precise and capable of empirical evaluation. Curiously enough, he did not include differential association theory, which is also capable of evaluation. Nonetheless, Downes's general conclusion was that there has been little progress in the sense that knowledge had not been accumulated by each superseding theory. Weaknesses had not been ironed out, and technical improvements had not occurred. Barbara Wootton would have been disappointed with these follow-up results, but they might have confirmed what she suspected, and probably feared.

These three selected areas of pathology, the Bowlby thesis, problem families and 12 criminological hypotheses, very much reflect the thinking at the time. In the 60 years or so since *Social Science and Social Pathology* was published, fashions have changed and new ways of thinking have emerged. The Bowlby thesis is no longer discussed, but 'problem families' are still part of the modern criminological narrative, although as Barbara Wootton said, the more general the theory, the more likely it will last. Most of those 12 criminological hypotheses listed in Barbara Wootton's study have been replaced but, according to David Downes, with no attempt to produce cumulative knowledge. Perhaps what remains is not so much what Barbara Wootton said as the way she went about things. She believed the only way to advance knowledge was through criticism, and in doing so offered a model to be followed, and a blueprint for future research.

What of producing that life of the offender? Have we advanced or are we still producing that 'framework of a life', rather than 'life itself'? In this respect, we seem to have been rather more successful, but not necessarily in the direction Barbara Wootton might approve of. The theories that followed her study, labelling, social control, subcultural etc., all breathed life into the offender, but without the necessary prerequisite of the scientific method. At the most extreme were the ethnomethodologists such as Irving Goffman, whose method was to describe events and the actions of those engaged in those events. His book *Asylums*[19] was the classic of its kind, describing the interactions of staff and patients in the mental hospital. It put life into the study but did so without concern for the scientific method advocated by Barbara Wootton; indeed, it was as far from her approach as one could possibly get. Goffman produced a life but he did not produce Barbara Wootton's form of science.

This is but one extreme example of the theories that followed *Social Science and Social Pathology*. There were others, less extreme in the sense that they were essentially descriptive rather than empirical in the way Barbara Wootton understood that term. As David Downes says, they would not be theories aimed at building up a store of knowledge, but separate attempts to explain some or specific features of criminal behaviour. Often they were interesting and opened up new avenues of thought. They may have breathed life, but they were not producing an accumulated set of knowledge.

The courts

Running alongside Barbara Wootton's own life as a researcher and public speaker and her many other activities were her duties as a magistrate. She sat in the adult and juvenile courts in the inner London area for about 50 years, and her book *Crime and Penal Policy*, which had the subtitle *Reflections on fifty years experience*, illustrates this.[20] She said this book was not written for the criminological experts but for the nonprofessional public with an interest in penology. Whether it reached that audience or not is difficult to say; it nevertheless contained a considerable amount of material that most criminological experts would have recognised and be happy to acknowledge. Her experience as a magistrate led her to reflect on the workings of the courts, the aims of criminal justice, including the practice of sentencing, and the outcome of those sentences.

She was also a member of the influential Streatfeild Committee,[21] an Interdepartmental Committee on the Business of the Criminal Courts, which reported in 1961. This Committee made two important recommendations, both of which can be seen as having within them the footprint and influence of Barbara Wootton. The main recommendations of the Streatfeild Committee were that courts should be made aware of the general results of relevant research, and courts should be supplied with fuller and better information about individual offenders. Both were central to Barbara's philosophy on sentencing.

Her writings, whether on *Social Science and Social Pathology* or otherwise, are littered with references to her experiences in the courts, some oblique, others less so. Her period as a magistrate was clearly important to her, if only because it brought her in touch with a class of people with whom she had hitherto little or no contact. Like for many others with a Labour Party philosophy of equality and an upper-middle-class background, it produced a slightly romantic vision of working-class life, even if there was genuine sympathy for the poverty and unfairness of a system which produces such inequalities. Her second husband George came from a working-class background, and Barbara says she was involved in his side of the family. When she was appointed a magistrate, she was 28 years of age, with little or no experience of life outside the confines of that upper-middle-class Edwardian background.

She was immediately made aware of some of the distinctive features of the Magistracy in England and Wales, what she saw as the amateurishness in the lower levels of the criminal justice system. No expertise was required or necessary for one's appointment, nor indeed was any previous interest in crime, the courts or criminal justice. Most appointments were made (and some still are) on a political basis rather than a demonstrative interest in criminality. Barbara herself was appointed on the recommendation of the St. Marylebone local Labour Party, of which she was a diligent supporter.[22]

Barbara Wootton noted the contrast in the personnel between the Magistrates Courts and Crown Courts, and differences in the style and practice of those passing sentence. Whereas those in the Magistrates Courts were amateurs, in the sense they were not trained lawyers, those in the Higher Courts were professionals – except of course the Stipendiary Magistrates, who were also trained lawyers. She thought it strange that whereas two or three people in the Magistrates Courts should participate in fixing the penalty for 'someone who has shoplifted a few groceries', only one individual was responsible for deciding on a maximum of life imprisonment for serious offences – again, the exception is the Stipendiary Magistrate, who sits alone but whose powers are of course limited to that of other magistrates.[23] Barbara Wootton seemed to believe that the decisions from one person, a trained lawyer, were somehow more questionable than those from two or more persons who were untrained. She was certainly suspicious of the way the lawyers, especially the senior judges, were recruited, as nearly all came from a specific social class (i.e., similar to that of her own!), producing what she thought as a correspondingly narrow vision. Their background, and the way they were protected from ordinary people, she said, creates the impression 'that these are not as other men are'.[24]

Indeed they are not, and according to Barbara Wootton, they are rather full of themselves. 'I cannot forbear from adding that the judiciary and the Bar between them are also addicted to a degree of self adulation which, in my experience, is unrivalled by any other profession.'[25] She thought this amount of self-congratulation was fostered by the 'cotton wool in which they are wrapped', and she wondered whether anyone could imagine architects or doctors talking like that. Perhaps not, but then architects or doctors are not required to create an impression of infallibility.

Then there is the jury system, which Barbara Wootton said was but another example of the use of amateurs in criminal justice, a system incidentally praised by de Tocqueville but criticised by others. Barbara saw the jury as an outcome of the adversarial system of justice which she seemed neither to approve of nor disapprove of, but accepted 'it is too firmly rooted in our history for there to be the slightest chance of substituting a more direct and rational method of searching for the truth.'[26] She noted, however, that there were handicaps under which juries are required to operate – they must come to a decision, in circumstances that are not made easy for them. They are, she said, required to perform fantastic feats of attention and memory in trials which may last for weeks, or even months, without the help of such elementary tools as facilities for note-taking or to hear recordings of evidence on which their memories may not be clear.[27]

In spite of these comments, her views on the jury system were surprisingly benign. Others have taken a more critical stance. Louis Blom-Cooper, for example, argues for the abandonment of the jury system on the grounds that it violates basic principles of justice; that is to say, jury members are not trained, do not have to give reasons for their decisions, are not required to show any interest in criminal justice matters and are not selected on the basis of any capability. He also says there is no evidence that their verdicts are better (i.e., more often correct) than when courts sit without them, as with the Diplock courts sitting in Northern Ireland during the Troubles.[28] Barbara Wootton notes that the system has come under criticism, but she makes no suggestions to reform or abandon it. She said it was impossible to assess its merits as long as we are kept in ignorance of what goes on in the jury room. This of course is only about their decisions; it does not meet Louis Blom-Cooper's other criticisms.

Yet overall, she seemed to support and favour the amateurism of English justice (the Scottish system is different) which usually involves three magistrates sitting together. She preferred that system to the use of the single Stipendiary Magistrate (now called District Judges). She thought lay magistrates provided a cheap system of justice – but incidentally not that cheap – but also believed that the system 'gives some safeguard against the individual prejudices to which we are all liable'.[29] She seems to discount the likelihood of a domineering magistrate imposing his/her will on less forceful colleagues, or of the equal likelihood of a bench of magistrates being swayed by the knowledge and experience of the Justices clerk, a trained lawyer. She did, however, accurately predict the declining use of the lay system, especially in the larger metropolitan areas – district judges being seen as more efficient in that they speed up the system and appear more receptive to change.

Sentencing and the tariff

Sentencing and the outcomes of sentences preoccupied Barbara Wootton. She devoted a Hamlyn Lecture to sentencing, and it appeared throughout many of her other writings. She asked basic questions such as 'What are the courts trying to do?' 'Are they there to punish the wicked, or prevent harm to others?' Barbara Wootton was a firm opponent of the former, and a firm supporter of the latter. She said, 'I do not think that it is our business to punish the wicked. Our business is to do what we can to prevent the repetition of crimes.'[30] The courts, she said, are there to pass sentences using the minimum action which can offer an adequate prospect of preventing further offences.[31]

This rather straightforward and openly Utilitarian view on the nature of the courts, and of punishment, is of course straight out of Bentham. It looks to the future by attempting to control action that is, the action of the offender and the action of others. Punishment and the infliction of pain (or producing unhappiness), said Bentham, is regrettable but necessary, yet only in sufficient amounts as to control actions. Too little, and it is not likely to be successful; too much, and it is unnecessary. Finding the right amount is an empirical question, an approach which of course directly appealed to Barbara Wootton. It allowed her to claim that Utilitarians tend to be penal reformers inasmuch as they hope that more intelligent and humane penal policies may produce better results.[32]

She was not, however, blind to the defects of a Utilitarian view. She cites the example where an offender might only mend his ways if he received better treatment from the court than he was likely to achieve in his ordinary life. 'And what good would that be for general deterrence?'[33] And deterring others was as important as deterring the individual offender. As a Utilitarian, Barbara Wootton obviously denied any relevance of a 'just deserts' philosophy with the attendant retributive theory of punishment. It was too subjective for her taste. 'Just deserts' involves inflicting punishment because the offender has deserved it, or in Kantian terms, because he had acted wickedly. The amount to be given was according to the gravity of the offence. Barbara recognised that it was a popular philosophy and a basic principle of the modern criminal law.[34] Yet it was contrary to her vision of sentencing.

Her answer to the question of the aims of sentencing was that sentences should be judged by their skill in preventing recidivism. She saw the operation of the current system as one which 'must surely be without parallel' in its defects[35] – some of which were embedded in theories of punishment, others more practical in the way the system was arranged. She listed five major defects.

First there was a lack of feedback available to the courts on the effectiveness of their judgements, for 'effectiveness' read 'success', and for 'success' read 'reconviction rates'.

Second, and linked to the first point, most magistrates had no idea as to the object of the exercise in which they were engaged. That is to say, there was no way of knowing about the guilt or innocence of those appearing before them, and no way of knowing whether the sentences imposed were successful or not in reducing crime. The only certain evidence came from the failures, that is, of those offenders who reappeared whether for a similar or different offence. In this respect, Barbara Wootton's conclusion was that her 50 years' or so experience had taught her much about many aspects of human behaviour, but provided no data on which she could either improve her own performance or advise others how they should improve theirs.[36]

Third, she returned to the point made earlier, that the more serious the decision, the more likely it is to be made by one man alone, rather than by a group in consultation. This she found strange, believing that better decisions are made by two or more people. She gave no further justification for this, presumably believing it to be self-evident.

Fourth, she also repeated the point that decisions were being made by untrained amateurs 'inasmuch as the subject of penology has no place in the training of judges or magistrates' – incidentally less so nowadays.

Finally, the courts have a wide discretion in the choice of sentences, but there are no explicit rules as to how that discretion should be exercised, nor indeed any explicit principles determining the object of that exercise.[37]

Her answer to the question of sentencing was straightforward: we should be moving towards a more scientific approach, with evidence of success or failure helping to determine the appropriate sentence. She turned again to the expectation that social science will one day help resolve the dilemmas. 'Science can undoubtedly examine the effects of sentences with a view to improving their future effectiveness in particular directions.' In contrast, she thought a retributive view leads us nowhere; it lies outside the field of scientific enquiry, where 'all the science in the world cannot measure whether a man has been punished as much as, or more, or less than he deserves.'[38]

Such a view brought her into direct conflict with a central platform of modern sentencing, i.e., its dependence on the tariff. The tariff is a rough and ready guide providing a measure of agreement about what is an appropriate sentence for a certain crime. Where a sentence is set outside the tariff – that is, it is either too severe or too lenient – the Court of Appeal will be expected to make the necessary adjustment. In that rough and ready way, the punishment fits the crime and accordingly approximates to a notion of justice. One of the major benefits of the tariff is that it is able to include numerous principles of sentencing, such as just deserts, reformation and deterrence, the latter involving individual deterrence and deterring others. Taken together, those principles help provide a measure of certainty, both to the offender and to society. And because it includes a retributive philosophy, offenders and nonoffenders alike know and can expect that a certain level of punishment will follow a certain offence. For illegal car-parking, the offence will not lead to imprisonment, but for armed robbery it certainly will. The tariff therefore provides an approximation to justice. Bentham had little time for justice, calling it an 'imaginary personage fit only for public discourse'. As a committed Utilitarian, Barbara Wootton would agree. Yet she knew that justice is likely to remain a platform upon which any philosophy of punishment will continue to operate and justice is contained within the tariff.

Barbara Wootton was not in favour of the tariff. She found support in the Streatfeild Committee, which thought the tariff had outstayed its usefulness, saying it can no longer be relied on to fit all the considerations in the court's mind.[39] The Committee also thought the tariff looked backward to the offence, whereas Courts, said Streatfeild, should be concerned with other matters, efficacy being one. That meant looking forward, which presumably also meant being more scientific. Unsurprisingly, Streatfeild thought research should be conducted on the basis that more information be made available to the courts.[40]

Barbara Wootton would agree on both these points, but then as a member of the Streatfeild Committee she probably wrote this bit of the Report anyway. She was certainly suspicious of the tariff. She had two major objections. First, she thought the tariff was biased too heavily towards the iniquity of crimes, i.e., retribution. Second, she suspected that assessments were made on the basis of wickedness, that is to say of the consequences of the offence and the offender's intentions, again on retribution, which she said time and time again were not capable of scientific verification.

Her suspicions centre around the ability to assess the state of the offender's mind and produce decisions based on those assessments. These matters are dealt with in greater detail in a later chapter; here I only want to make the point that Barbara Wootton thought that the tariff contained moral evaluations which she said are inherently subjective; no subsequent experience can prove them right or wrong.[41]

A scientific approach to sentencing

Barbara Wootton talked much of a scientific approach to sentencing but said little about what that would look like. And would it be acceptable if introduced? She considers this in her Hamlyn Lectures and argues that a prerequisite would be for more data on the effectiveness of decisions. But again she said little about what would that data consist of. Should there be more about the offender's background?

Already, considerable information is provided to the courts. Some comes from the offenders themselves, where their presence in the witness box gives the courts some indication of the offender's character. Other comes from the police, who provide some details of the offender's background, including employment record and previous convictions. If more is required, the court can ask for a social enquiry report from the probation service (or social services department if the offender is a juvenile) or from the medical and psychiatric services.

Does this information by the police, probation and psychiatric services help to improve or make more efficient (read, scientific) sentencing? The Streatfeild Committee considered these questions. Their Report gave no answers as to the scientific merit, presumably because in the current state of knowledge none was available. What it did was to provide guidance on the nature of these reports. It said that reports should *inter alia* contain information about the offender's background, the offender's culpability and about how the offender's criminal career could be checked.

Does this information assist the court to make better decisions? And if not, what is missing? Barbara Wootton acknowledged that the reports had little scientific merit in the form currently presented. Their merit was otherwise. She said they helped fill the enormous gap that separates those on the Bench from those standing in the dock, but she was pessimistic about their value as an aid to sentencing, and reducing crime. She noted too that preparation of these reports was 'more characteristic of the persons concerned in the operation', i.e., were as much a reflection of the report writers' views as they were of the offender. She also said that she 'welcomed social enquiry reports because they make me feel cosy inasmuch as they transform a "case" into a human being; but sadly I am driven to the conclusion . . . that they do little to make me (or anybody else) a better sentencer'.[42] For psychiatric reports in the juvenile courts, she was even more critical, asking, where was the evidence in those reports of psychiatric expertise? She thought they could, almost without exception, have been written by anyone sympathetic to children.

Although she spoke often of a 'scientific approach to sentencing', it was never clear what that would mean. What was required in those Reports which could bring them closer to that scientific approach? Neither Barbara Wootton nor the Streatfeild Report provided answers, except perhaps to say better information was required on the effectiveness of respective sentences.

Nor was it clear how a scientific approach would fit the traditions and philosophy of the modern court system. Barbara Wootton seemed aware of some of the contradictions and the implications of her scientific approach, yet still maintained its worth. She retained her belief that a reductionist approach to sentencing was sufficient and the way forward. However, it led her into strange and awkward territory, first in terms of the way sentencing may affect the Durkheimian view of offending the collective conscience, and second in that it would move the court toward more indeterminate sentences.

In the first, assume more data is available and able to provide a measure of certainty about the sentence required to reduce reoffending for a particularly serious crime. Assume too that it provides or suggests that in this case a certain type of serious offence would for this particular offender not require a lengthy sentence because it was not necessary for a reduction in future criminality. Accordingly, the court could conclude that, say, a probation order would be sufficient. Or perhaps consider the converse, that a less serious offence would require a considerably more serious punishment in order to prevent future criminality. What then? How would that be received generally? The answer of course is that it would offend elementary notions of the tariff and of justice. In Durkheim's terms, it would offend the collective conscience.

Emile Durkheim argued that crime wounds the collective conscience, especially serious crimes; the function of punishment was to heal it and restore its equilibrium. If the punishment was too light or too severe, the collective sentiments were not healed. Failure to heal would lead to a sense of distrust of the courts and the legal system generally, and open the way for social disruption.[43] Admittedly, terms like 'collective conscience' or 'collective sentiments' are imprecise, as is the assertion that the collective sentiments can be identified and seen to not be healed if the sentence is too light or too heavy. But tucked within that Durkheim argument is an important point, that we do feel aggrieved if a sentence is too light and/or too heavy. An appropriate sentence, almost certainly aligned with the tariff, does restore equilibrium. Ignore this and disequilibrium follows, producing a situation more serious than the failure to sentence according to scientific principles.

In the second of Barbara Wootton's Hamlyn Lectures,[44] there is the suggestion that custodial sentences should be indeterminate. She said, 'If the primary object of a sentence is to discourage further offences . . . the offender's release can hardly be forecast in advance; in must depend on his progress.' She recognises that indeterminate sentences have not been popular, the offenders do not like them (nor should they), and neither do the prison authorities. To these could be added all those concerned with civil liberties. She recognises too that in the state of knowledge about what should be the appropriate penal treatment leading to the appropriate date of release, our knowledge is scanty. Accordingly, 'indeterminacy does I think demand safeguards.'[45] Indeed it does. Two safeguards are suggested, that the court should fix the maximum period of detention (if so we are back to the tariff), and decisions as to detention or release should be made by those who have face-to-face contact with the offender.

It is not the purpose here to evaluate arguments about indeterminate sentencing, and Barbara Wootton is correct in saying there are increasing numbers of indeterminate sentences in the legal calendar, but the dangers are clear and obvious: it is an unfair system, open to enormous abuse, and based on the assumption that the authorities making the decision have some measure of expertise. The point to be made here is different; it is that Barbara Wootton was led into this position as a logical extension of her argument about the scientific nature of sentencing and her dismissal of the tariff and all associated with that. Takeaway notions of justice, fairness and deserts and the logical corollary is the indeterminate sentence with all the dangers that implies. If the aim is solely to reduce offending, as opposed to providing a just system, then indeterminacy is the obvious result.

Barbara Wootton was of course not wholly unaware of some of the pitfalls. She recognised that the various objectives of sentencing as they operate at present are mutually incompatible. There is no sentence yet devised that can at one and the same time protect the public, punish the offender, reform him, deter him and discourage others from committing similar offences. She recognises too that different responses arise from different sentences; some offenders respond to a punitive sentence, and others do not. Some are able to be reformed; others are not. Her solution at this stage of our knowledge for those passing sentence must be to make a choice between different objectives and arrange them in order of priority. If this is not a wholly satisfactory solution, then as Barbara Wootton says, it at least makes clear the nature and reasons for the decisions made, and hopefully presents an intelligible explanation to others, including the offender.[46]

Juvenile justice and the juvenile court

Barbara Wootton's criticisms of the courts were more of a commentary than a critique, but it was to children and the then juvenile justice system to which she gave most of her attention. A great deal of the chapter in her Autobiography entitled 'Magistrate' was given over to juvenile crime and juvenile justice. She wrote often about 'Young Offenders', and it was the juvenile justice system which she thought required the most radical overhaul.

She said of the juvenile court that she 'hopes for the day when the social and moral training of all children will be regarded as a matter of educational not penal concern'. That is to say, all juvenile courts and all the apparatus of delinquent children of school age should be swept away so that 'any child whose behaviour causes concern will be referred to his school'.[47] She goes on to say, 'Only when every child sees that his future is in the hands of the parents and teachers that he knows . . . shall we be able to claim that children are no longer treated as criminals.'[48]

Incidentally, one wonders how much her views on juvenile justice were affected by her own personal position. Her contact with children over many years was mainly as a magistrate and a peer. It was based on a practical knowledge of their problems, not on close emotional contact, which, according to one of her friends, produced a distanced and unrealistic view. It may have been this that helps explain her radical proposal, that erring children should not be treated in the criminal justice system but by the educational system.[49] She often asserted, but without much evidence, that the education system was the appropriate place to deal with delinquency, it being a problem of faulty education. She said criminality of the young was a failure of the system. Accordingly, you should not punish children for such failures.[50]

Barbara Wootton had three objections to the then–juvenile courts (now replaced by Youth Courts, but still retaining many of the features to which she objected): First, what she calls the 'legal mumbo jumbo' of the courts, which she says appears ridiculous to children. 'Procedural absurdities', she calls them. Second, that children do not learn from strangers, but from the climate in which they spend their lives, i.e., parents, school etc. Third, that courts stamp the child with a delinquent label[51] – hence the need to replace courts with an educational system where a number of counsellors attached to the schools would be available to work with the teachers on issues which are important to children at the time. More serious matters, including delinquency, would be dealt with by an informed discussion with a child, his parents, the teachers and counsellors. This so-called comprehensive conference might have to decide that a delinquent's best chance would be to remain in the community, or perhaps be sent away to attend a special school. Barbara Wootton accepted that 'in other words it would exercise virtually the same functions as do the juvenile courts', but, she said, 'with the important difference that the conference would no longer rank as a juvenile court . . . but would be composed of people known to the children'.[52]

Her proposal was similar to the Children's Panel in Scotland, introduced after the Kilbrandon Report. Barbara Wootton acknowledged that there were similarities but thought there were important differences. Her proposals, she said, centred around the education system, whereas the panels in Scotland more closely resembled the old-style juvenile court. Nonetheless, it is clear the Wootton proposals would face similar problems as the panel system. It seems some things don't change. For irrespective of any hopes there may be about changing the system, Scottish Panels deal with similar children as before and send away to penal institutions similar children as before. Moreover, in the panel system objections still come from the child and family when the child is sent away. And there are still objections that the panel making the decision fails to represent and understand the child's difficulties. It seems too that panel members come from very much the same background as the magistrates they replaced, i.e., mainly middle class, and however much the panel tries to do otherwise, the delinquent label is still applied. It seems that whatever name is used, panel or juvenile court, the basic problem remains: that one group has the power and makes the decisions, and the other has none and does not. Nonetheless, in one respect the panel system does closely resemble Barbara Wootton's ideal; it is possible to have debates and discussion between panel members, the offender and his family in ways not possible under a more formal court system.

That apart, it remains a moot point that the child sent away from home by a Comprehensive Conference would find it more acceptable and be less hostile to the system than if sent by a juvenile court. It seems too that whatever name is given to the decision, call it treatment, care or whatever, the child will see the decision as punishment. And what of the situation where parents object to the Conference's decision? Barbara Wootton's solution was an appeal system, not to a formal court, but along the lines of a tribunal, usually comprised of laymen but with a legally qualified chairman, 'one who was associated with many facets of our social services'.[53] How does this differ from the present system? Hardly at all.

Barbara Wootton's proposal for a Comprehensive Conference must face similar criticisms as have been directed at the Scottish panel system, at least in its early stages. Critics of the panel-type system argued that removing the juvenile court also removes the child's procedural rights guaranteed by the court system. Barbara Wootton's response is that children have fewer rights than adults anyway, and removing those that still exist matters less than dealing with children in a more appropriate setting. Other criticisms are that changing the label obscures the nature of the enterprise; a panel is still a court in all but name, only with a greater pretence to be acting in the offender's interests. And a panel within the education system is unrealistic; teachers will not want to be involved in decisions which involve sending children away from home. A final criticism would be that modern types of criminality, such as those involving substance abuse, make a panel system unworkable; or if not, then unrealistic.

Her proposal was radical in that it sets out to reshape the juvenile justice system, and do away with the business of the traditional juvenile court. The proposal, however, came to nothing. There was little support and little enthusiasm for such changes. It was certainly ill timed. It came too late, or rather it came at a time when there was a changing mood on juvenile delinquency. This was largely as a result of the murder of James Bulger, aged two, on 12 February 1993, an offence which changed forever public views in Britain about juvenile crime and juvenile justice. It certainly changed the pictures of juvenile offenders, where before it was inconceivable that children were capable of such criminality. Introducing a panel-type system would be seen immediately as offering a less secure system and, rightly or wrongly, heralding in a more permissive approach.

It seems too that Barbara Wootton's views on juvenile justice were based on a view of children as always being the victims, which nowadays appears slightly unrealistic, if not slightly romantic. Current levels of juvenile violence promote a different view. No one doubts that children are children, whatever they have done, but to suggest that parents and schools would be the most suitable environs in which to assess and decide on future outcomes is part of that unrealistic picture. The modern view, which sees the juvenile offender as having a range of problems, in some case severe and multiple – and some due to the failures of the education system itself – requires a different approach than that envisioned by Barbara Wootton. There would be a reluctance to move away from a traditional court system, believing that would lessen the impact on offenders.

The penal system

Barbara Wootton's examination of the penal system was mainly in terms of commenting on legal changes such as the introduction of parole, changes to the jury system (which involved introducing majority verdicts), changes to committal proceedings in Magistrates Courts whereby offenders are committed to the High Courts for trial, and the introduction of new sentences such as the Suspended Sentence. Most of these changes had been made under the 1967 Criminal Justice Act. She had a chapter in the book *Crime and Penal Policy* devoted to custodial sentences, but as she did not conduct empirical research of her own, it was to others that she referred.

Interestingly enough, Barbara Wootton said nothing about women in prison. Yet in 2017 there were 3,994 women in prison in England and Wales, and the number has more than doubled since 1993, with an increase of nearly 2,300. Many women in prison have high levels of mental health problems and histories of abuse, and there have been increases in the numbers of self-inflicted deaths and self-harm in this group. Again, if only to repeat the point, it is curious that someone interested in the position of women generally should appear to have ignored women's fate within prisons. Nor, incidentally, did she say anything about women as prison officers or prison governors (or even as police officers), even though she spent a considerable amount of time as a visitor in Holloway – a women's prison.

Her views on the probation service are interesting, if only because she does not make the same criticisms as she did of social workers, or place probation officers in the same category as social workers, although they saw themselves as social workers of the courts. She does not appear to notice that their training was of the same 'pretentious rubbish' that was given to social workers (more of this in another chapter) in that they were trained to practise the same form of casework which she so heavily criticised. She also fell into the trap described by George Mair as seeing probation officers as beyond reproach, which helped lead them into the position in which they found themselves, i.e., a service under Transforming Rehabilitation, which divided it between a National Probation Service and a privatised system run by Community Rehabilitation Corporations.[54] In his assessment of the Probation Service, George Mair (2016) thought that probation always believed it was on the side of the angels and that its staff were 'the good guys' of the criminal justice system. He said that meant it tended to be somewhat complacent. He also thought that a good deal of research has been complicit in this, so that criminologists, and this includes Barbara Wootton, have never subjected probation to the same levels of criticism that the police, prison officers or sentencers have had to face[55] – the implication being that this form of protection, akin to political correctness, had done the Probation Service no favours. Rather, he thought it had been damaging, leaving the service without the ability to help itself in the battle to survive.

There is something to be said in favour of Mair's critique. There are numerous examples where the Probation Service has seen itself as 'on the side of the angels', believing it was operating for the best in an otherwise uncertain world – or if not, then wanting to stand aloof from some of the more morally unattractive, yet realistic, features of the criminal justice system. It never sought collaboration with the prison or police service, seeing the former as 'punitive' and the latter as 'authoritarian', and in doing so held a lofty detachment from them. Criminologists including Barbara Wootton have helped foster the image of a self-righteous service. She said, 'A more dedicated company of men and women than those employed in the probation service it would be hard to find in any profession.'[56] Such comments, if not actively promoting self-righteousness, then at least have not challenged or attacked it. The result, according to Mair, is a service built on 'shaky foundations' leading to what he calls 'a narrative of loss'.[57] Did Barbara Wootton put aside her usual critical gaze when it came to the probation service? It seems so, although as shown earlier she had a fairly low opinion of the value of probation reports.

Her views on other aspects of the adult system were conventional. She supported the increased use of what she calls 'civilising influences' such as the new educational facilities and opportunities for prisoners to undertake academic degrees from the Open University. She supported too the increasing use of aftercare, thereby 'bridging the gap between imprisonment and return to the world outside'.[58] She does not lament the loss of 'Corrective Training' or 'Preventative Detention', devised in 1948 to keep the 'wicked and dangerous out of harm's way for long periods', which turned out to be nothing more than a way of increasing the length of the sentence as no special or extra training was ever given.[59]

All this was in line with a typical liberal tradition. She was of course writing at a time when prisons were quite different from what they are today (2019). Then, the prison population in England and Wales was around 40,000 – compared with 80,000 nowadays, and when there were fewer problems of drugs in prisons – the full impact of the drug problem was still a decade or so away. More importantly, the prison staff then were not faced with levels of violence that exist today, whether the violence of prisoner on prisoner or prisoner on staff.[60]

Contributions to parliamentary debates

Barbara Wootton spoke in many debates in the House of Lords, some specifically on criminological topics but often on others of more general interest. In between her first speech on 4 February 1959 and her last on 4 July 1985, she is recorded as having made 1,790 contributions to House of Lords debates, her most significant speeches covering crime and drugs. She spoke on drug offences, noting the hysterical reaction which met the 'Cannabis' Report (see Chapter 3), seeing it as occurring 'when the public senses that some critical and objective study threatens to block an outlet for indulgence in the pleasures of moral indignation'.[61]

She also spoke on a range of criminological and noncriminological matters. For example, she spoke on corporal punishment in schools on the Education (Corporal Punishment) Bill, saying, 'We are thinking of what would be a serious criminal assault if similar and equal force was applied to an attack made upon a grown adult of equal size.'[62] She asked questions about crimes of conspiracy, and spoke on so called 'sus' offences where she sought an identifiable activity on behalf of the offender and not just that he looked suspicious of committing an offence. She spoke against sending prostitutes to prison, saying a community service order was to be preferred.[63] She spoke also on the Incurable Patients Bill, the purpose of which was to protect incurable patients from avoidable suffering and to strengthen their rights. The principle behind the Bill was that the disposal of a patient's life in the extreme circumstances specified was a matter for the patient alone. Barbara Wootton was a keen supporter meeting the objections that it was the wrong time – 'it is never the right time', she said – that we have hospices – 'not enough', she said – and that we should train more doctors and nurses to treat such patients – 'it takes too long', she said.[64]

One of the most important contributions was on the debate on capital punishment, when in 1965 she moved the Second Reading of the Murder (Abolition of the Death Penalty) Bill.[65] This bill was aimed at amending the Homicide Act 1957, which retained the death penalty for murder committed under five categories. They were murder in the furtherance of theft, when resisting arrest or resisting the assistance of some person who is helping in arrest, murder of a police or prison officer, or any second or repeated murder. The 1957 Act itself was a compromise to proposals for the abolition of the death penalty; this bill would repeal those conditions. Barbara Wootton in her speech pointed out that many of these compromises had not worked: they had produced numerous injustices and anomalies. She said the Homicide Act 1957 did not enact the death penalty for the poisoner, the sex murderer or the murderer of small children. The aim was to deter the professional criminal, but many who have suffered death as a result of the legislation were not professional criminals. She gave a number of examples such as that of a college lecturer, aged 33, who murdered a girl and her boyfriend in a passion of sexual jealousy, who had one previous conviction for homosexuality. He, like a number of others, could not be called a professional criminal.

She used the research by Thorsten Sellin to support her arguments. Sellin examined the fluctuations in the murder rate over a number of years in many US states and many countries in Europe where the death penalty had been abolished and sometimes retained. His conclusion was that although there were short-term fluctuations in the rates, it was impossible to draw any inferences that there is a visible and tangible long-term relationship between the use of the death penalty and the murder rate. Barbara Wootton saw this research as giving compelling support to her arguments.

It was a speech, short and to the point, emphasising the risks in abolition, but emphasising too the moral dimension involved whereby the state is involved in judicial killing. The motion was passed; the effect of the bill was to provide an automatic life sentence of imprisonment for any conviction of murder, a legal position which still applies some 50 years or so later. How much this was due to Barbara Wootton is difficult to say, but being responsible for moving the motion for the bill's second reading must have had an effect.

Her views on the death penalty were clear. Her personal objection was moral; she said to deprive another person of life is inherently an immoral action, which is degrading to those that perform them and most conspicuously true of judicial execution, and second, that there remains the risk that a mistake can be made and that an innocent man can be convicted and hanged. She quoted Lafayette's declaration that he would continue to demand the abolition of the death penalty until he had the infallibility of human judgement demonstrated to him. Her presentation was forceful, clear and to the point. Moreover, criminologists have rarely had the luxury of someone to represent them in such august circles.

From the reaction of other Members, Baroness Wootton of Abinger was a respected member, recognised as someone able to make a powerful contribution to debates. It is curious, therefore, that she thought so little of her contributions.

A concluding thought

Barbara Wootton said of the penal system,

> I have become increasingly haunted by the image . . . of the whole penal system as in a sense a gigantic irrelevance – wholly misconceived as a method of controlling phenomena the origins of which are inextricably rooted in the structure of society.

Could it be that she is correct? Might it be that the penal system is a gigantic irrelevance, whereby crime rates rise and fall independently of actions taken by various aspects of the penal system? If that is so, and I strongly suspect she is right, the aim of the penal system is not about controlling actions, or producing various measures of rehabilitation, but simply to take offenders out of the system and give some relief to society. It does not mean always sending them to prison or any other custodial setting, but to finding ways which promote different ways of acting or behaving. These might include spending time on probation or community service, or other ways of providing relief to others. It is not a solution likely to have general appeal, but it does suggest a way of thinking which is more realistic, and therefore less optimistic and less likely to be a failure.

Notes

1 Wootton B (1967) *In a World I Never Made. Autobiographical Reflections*. George Allen and Unwin p. 105.
2 Oakley A. (2011) A *Critical Woman*. Bloomsbury Academic p. 220.
3 Wootton B (1959) *Social Science and Social Pathology*. George Allen and Unwin p. 16.
4 Bowlby J (1946) *Forty Four Juvenile Thieves*. Balliere, Tindall and Cox.
5 Wootton B (1959) *Social Science and Social Pathology*. George Allen and Unwin. op. cit.
6 Ibid. p. 146.
7 Ibid. p. 154.

8 Ibid. p. 156.
9 Wootton B (1962) *A Social Scientists Approach to Maternal Deprivation in Deprivation of Maternal Care; A Reassessment of Its Effects*. WHO pp. 63–73.
10 Wootton B (1959) *Social Science and Social Pathology*. George Allen and Unwin. op. cit. p. 54.
11 Ibid. p. 62.
12 Ibid. p. 301.
13 Downes D. (1986) Back to basics: Reflections on Barbara Wootton's 'twelve criminological hypotheses' In Bean PT. and Whynes D (eds) *Barbara Wootton. Social Science and Public Policy. Essays in her Honour*. Tavistock pp. 195–215.
14 These quotes are from Wootton B (1959) *Social Science and Social Pathology*. George Allen and Unwin. op. cit. pp. 83, 134.
15 Ibid. p. 316.
16 Ibid. pp. 316–317.
17 Ibid. p. 320.
18 Downes D (1986) Back to basics: Reflections on Barbara Wootton's 'twelve criminological hypotheses' In Bean PT. and Whynes D (eds) *Barbara Wootton. Social Science and Public Policy. Essays in her Honour*. Tavistock. op. cit. p. 198.
19 Goffman E (1961) *Asylums*. Penguin.
20 Wootton B (1978) *Crime and Penal Policy; Reflections on Fifty Years Experience*. Allen and Unwin.
21 HMSO (1961) *Interdepartmental Committee on the Business of the Criminal Courts* (the Streatfeild Committee).
22 Wootton B (1975/1992) The Administration of justice. Lecture given to the University of Leeds. Reprinted In Seal V and Bean P (eds) *Barbara Wootton Selected Writings Vol. 1 Crime and the Penal System* pp. 95–108.
23 Wootton B (1978) *Crime and Penal Policy; Reflections on Fifty Years Experience*. Allen and Unwin. op. cit. p. 77.
24 Ibid. p. 81.
25 Ibid.
26 Ibid. p. 81.
27 Ibid. p. 101.
28 See Blom-Cooper L (2015) *Power of Persuasion*. Hart Publishing.
29 Wootton B (1975/1992) The Administration of Justice. Lecture given to the University of Leeds. Reprinted In Seal V and Bean P (eds) *Barbara Wootton Selected Writings Vol. 1 Crime and the Penal System*. op. cit. p. 106.
30 She made this point time and again. It was a central platform to her debate with Professor Hart. See Wootton B (1963) *Crime and the Criminal Law: Reflections of a Magistrate and a Social Scientist*. (The Hamlyn Lectures) Stevens and Sons. (Second Edition 1981 with postscripts to each chapter) pp. 32–57.
31 Wootton B (1963) *Crime and the Criminal Law: Reflections of a Magistrate and a Social Scientist*. (The Hamlyn Lectures) Stevens and Sons. (Second Edition 1981 with postscripts to each chapter). op. cit. p. 95.
32 Ibid. p. 97.
33 Ibid.
34 Wootton B (1967) *In a World I Never Made. Autobiographical Reflections*. George Allen and Unwin. op. cit. p. 242.

35 Wootton B (1963) *Crime and the Criminal Law: Reflections of a Magistrate and a Social Scientist*. (The Hamlyn Lectures) Stevens and Sons. (Second Edition 1981 with postscripts to each chapter). op. cit. pp. 91, 103.
36 Ibid. p. 107.
37 Ibid. p. 91.
38 Ibid. pp. 94–95.
39 HMSO (1961) *Interdepartmental Committee on the Business of the Criminal Courts* (the Streatfeild Committee). op. cit. para 262–263.
40 Ibid. para 269.
41 Wootton B (1975/1992) The Administration of Justice. Lecture given to the University of Leeds. Reprinted In Seal V and Bean P (eds) *Barbara Wootton Selected Writings Vol. 1 Crime and the Penal System*. op. cit. p. 94.
42 Wootton B (1963) *Crime and the Criminal Law: Reflections of a Magistrate and a Social Scientist*. (The Hamlyn Lectures) Stevens and Sons. (Second Edition 1981 with postscripts to each chapter). op. cit. p. 45.
43 Durkheim E (1964) *The Division of Labour in Society*. Free Press.
44 Wootton B (1963) *Crime and the Criminal Law: Reflections of a Magistrate and a Social Scientist*. (The Hamlyn Lectures) Stevens and Sons. (Second Edition 1981 with postscripts to each chapter). op. cit. pp. 112–113.
45 Ibid. p. 113.
46 Wootton B (1967) *In a World I Never Made. Autobiographical Reflections*. George Allen and Unwin. op. cit. p. 240.
47 Ibid. p. 227.
48 Ibid. p. 228.
49 Oakley A. (2011) *A Critical Woman*. Bloomsbury Academic. op. cit. pp. 352–353.
50 Ibid. p. 255.
51 Wootton B (1978) *Crime and Penal Policy; Reflections on Fifty Years Experience*. Allen and Unwin. op. cit. See Chapter 9 especially pp. 173–174.
52 Ibid. p. 178.
53 Ibid. p. 180.
54 Bean PT (2019) *Probation and Privatisation*. Routledge p. 85.
55 Mair G (2016) "A difficult trip I think." The end days of the probation service in England and Wales? *European Journal of Probation* Vol. 8 No.1 pp. 3–15.
56 Wootton B (1963) *Crime and the Criminal Law: Reflections of a Magistrate and a Social Scientist*. (The Hamlyn Lectures) Stevens and Sons. (Second Edition 1981 with postscripts to each chapter). op. cit. p. 45.
57 Mair G (2016) "A difficult trip I think." The end days of the probation service in England and Wales? *European Journal of Probation* Vol. 8 No.1. op. cit. p. 6.
58 Wootton B (1978) *Crime and Penal Policy; Reflections on Fifty Years Experience*. Allen and Unwin. op. cit. p. 106.
59 Ibid. p. 104.
60 Some of the current problems are spelt out in the Prison Reform Trust annual report for 2017. In that year, a total of 344 prisoners died in custody, 113, or about one-third, of whose deaths were self-inflicted. There were 6,844 assaults on staff in the past two years, with 789 classified as serious. There were also changes to the prison population, an important one being an increase in the use of indeterminate sentences. More and more prisoners do not know when they might be released. Indeterminate sentences now

account for 14% of the sentenced prison population, an increase of 9% from 25 or so years ago. That means in 2017 there were 10,803 people currently serving an indeterminate sentence, 7,275 serving a life sentence and a further 3,528 serving an indeterminate sentence for public protection. Those serving a life sentence are also spending more of their sentence in prison. On average in 2017, they spend 16 years in custody, up from 13 years in 2001. There has also been a rise in the number of foreign nationals (non–UK passport holders) in prisons in England and Wales, currently making up 11% of the prison population, i.e., 9,791 foreign nationals in prison as of 31 March 2017, all of which increases tensions within the prison system and poses additional problems for staff and prisoners alike. Prison Reform Trust (2017) *Briefings. The Facts.*

61 House of Lords *Hansard* March 26 1969 col. 1306.
62 Ibid. col. 1321.
63 Ibid. 1 February 1977 Vol 379 col. 773.
64 House of Lords *Hansard* February 12 1973 cols. 226–301.
65 Oakley A (2011) *A Critical Woman*. Bloomsbury Academic p. 264.

References for publications by Barbara Wootton

Wootton B (1950) *Testament for Social Science*. George Allen and Unwin.

Wootton B (1959) *Social Science and Social Pathology*. George Allen and Unwin.

Wootton B (1962) *A Social Scientists Approach to Maternal Deprivation in Deprivation of Maternal Care; A Reassessment of Its Effects*. WHO pp. 63–73.

Wootton B (1963) *Crime and the Criminal Law: Reflections of a Magistrate and a Social Scientist* (The Hamlyn Lectures) Stevens and Sons. (Second Edition 1981 with postscripts to each chapter).

Wootton B (1967) *In a World I Never Made. Autobiographical Reflections*. George Allen and Unwin.

Wootton B (1975) The administration of justice. Lecture given to the University of Leeds. Reprinted In Seal V and Bean P (eds) *Barbara Wootton Selected Writings Vol. 1 Crime and the Penal System* pp. 95–108.

Wootton B (1978) *Crime and Penal Policy; Reflections on Fifty Years Experience*. Allen and Unwin.

Chapter 3

Crime and the criminal law

In this chapter, I want to examine Barbara Wootton's views on the extent of criminality in Britain – this meant England and Wales; she said little of the extent of crime elsewhere. Then I want to look at matters relating to the criminal law. I have included sections on the Wootton Report on Cannabis,[1] which was *inter alia* aimed at recasting existing drugs legislation, and the Report on Non Custodial Penalties.[2]

Crime in England and Wales

Barbara Wootton wrote frequently on the extent of criminality in England and Wales, noting the changing patterns and commenting on recent developments. She did not say a great deal that was new, but she offered a certain perspective, and wrote with clarity. She was of course writing at a time when few others were commenting on the criminal statistics.

What she said of youth crime was fairly standard, well known and straightforward, i.e., that the then–criminal statistics showed that the peak age of crime was 14, and the peak age group was 14 to 17. This was followed by the 18–21 age group, then the 22–25 group and so on. As far back as the early 19th century, commentators had talked of this being the peak age for criminality, followed by the 18 to 21 group, etc. Incidentally, there is now (2019) an unexplained increase in offending and imprisonment in the over-55 age group, mainly of serious offenders, a feature unknown in Barbara Wootton's day.

Various theories have been used to explain that peak age of crime, which unsurprisingly has often been linked to the educational system. One of these theories is related to the school-leaving age. So, in the late 1950s when the school-leaving age went to 15, the peak age followed that, having previously been aged 14. This led some theorists to suggest that crime was an expression of the insecurity relating to leaving school.[3]

It was never clear why crime should be so related, and why insecurity rather than any other factor was relevant, but this was a popular theory at the time. Barbara Wootton, however, was more interested in theories linking crime to truancy and to educational attainment, which she suspected had more relevance. Her suspicions were that juvenile offenders were more likely to be truants, and less likely to be successful educationally, but at the time there was little evidence to show that those were also more likely to be recidivists.[4] It was much later that a more direct link was established. She noted too, but made little comment, that a better predictor of criminality was in the number of court appearances. A Home Office booklet entitled *The Sentence of the Court* produced in 1964 showed that the best predictors of criminality in the younger age group were the number of previous convictions, and the age at those convictions. That is to say, the younger they were when first convicted and the more often they were convicted, the more likely they were to be reconvicted.

She noted too that crime was related to gender in that it was primarily a product of masculinity. At the time Barbara Wootton was writing, the ratio of male to female recorded crime was 7:1.[5] It has since changed (2019) to 4.5:1, undergoing a steady decline over the years. Again, there was nothing new in her comments on the crime ratios – the gender ratio had been well known – but it led Barbara Wootton to suggest, in what has now become a famous comment on female criminality, that if men behaved like women, and boys behaved like girls, the courts would be idle and the prisons empty.

As said in the previous chapter, she said little of women's criminality generally. She did, however, believe it improbable that differences in the crime rates were of biological origin. She referred to female criminality in the methodology section *of Social Science and Social Pathology* when she discussed the impact of the broken home on delinquency. She said broken homes must have fallen with roughly equal frequency on boys and girls. 'Yet no one asks why one sex should be nearly eight times more resistant to these shocks than the other.'[6] This comment was part of her attack on what she referred to as the prejudice that makes us curiously blind to the obvious. She noted how the myth was perpetuated that whereas 'boys seem to express their unhappiness by delinquent acts girls seem to find an outlet for theirs in sex' – a proposition she said was 'at variance with the facts'. In a typical Barbara Wootton flourish, she pointed to simple biological facts that in the sexual acts to which the girls are said to be prone, a girl normally requires the cooperation of a male partner.

What she said of female criminality was mainly to ask questions of a general nature. She suspected that some process of cultural conditioning must be at work in the one sex from which the other was everywhere exempt. She asked if female resistance to criminal temptations was due to internal or external sanctions. She asked also if women have a stronger moral sense and suffer more from the pangs of conscience, 'or was it just that they are more timid and dare not therefore risk the possible consequences of getting into trouble?'[7] Yet she added, 'To identify this would make possible a larger reduction in criminality than is offered by any other line of inquiry.'[8] However, she lamented on what she saw as the growing incidence of aggressive female behaviour, saying that women deserved the name of the gentler sex, 'for gentleness seems to be a greatly underestimated virtue'. She added, 'yet when I see women lusting after corporal and capital punishment I wonder sadly if there is much to choose between one sex and the other.'[9]

She also considered the impact on crime of the then-changing position of women generally and on what she called 'the mass exodus of women, especially married women from their homes into outside employment'. This was a new phenomenon in the Britain of the late 1950s and early 1960s. Could this change produce an increase in criminality, as the containment of women in the home seems to have accounted for their modest contribution hitherto? 'Why do they not copy or share their husbands' and colleagues stealing?'[10] No immediate answer seems forthcoming.

A third feature of the then patterns of criminality was the motoring offender. She said,

> In half a century the invention of the internal combustion machine has completely revolutionised the business of our criminal courts. The typical criminal of today is not the thief, nor the thug who hits an old lady over the head in order to possess himself of her handbag or to ransack her house; the typical offender is the motorist.[11]

In this respect, she was saying something that was new, or rather she belonged to a very small number of commentators making similar points. Her comments came at a time when there was little or no research on the motoring offender *per se*, and those who were drawing attention to this matter were often ignored. Trevor Willett was an exception. He had earlier begun to ask questions about the criminal background of motoring offender, especially the persistent motoring offender, and those committing serious motoring offences including drunken driving. Did they differ from other offenders in terms of their sociodemographic profile or extent of previous convictions? Willett had shown how the persistent motoring offender bore striking similarities in background and criminal record with other persistent offenders, often having an extensive criminal record in addition to motoring convictions. Willett's book was a revelation, changing contemporary ways of thinking. Barbara Wootton continued the campaign. It was the

> attitude to the motoring offenders of the large and influential public which simply does not look on these offences as crimes at all. And it is this attitude with all the moral values that this implies, and all the death and destruction for which it is responsible, that I wish to challenge.[12]

And challenge she did. She brought to public attention not simply of the numbers of offenders, but in a way they were given preference in the criminal justice system. First, she noted that the official criminal statistics did not include the offence of causing death by reckless driving within the category of homicides, although convictions for dangerous driving regularly exceeded the annual total for murder, all forms of manslaughter and infanticide put together.[13] For example, in 1955 the number of persons known to have been murdered was 113, and the number killed on the roads was 5,526.

Then there were the sentences passed on motoring offenders. She compared the numbers of motoring offenders convicted of reckless or dangerous driving who were sent to prison by the then-Assizes in 1955, with those sent to prison for crimes against property, without violence. The figures were 31% and 67% respectively. And for offenders in the High Court convicted of drunken driving, only 13% were sent to prison. Also in the Magistrates Courts, 'the tenderness towards the motoring offender is even more striking', where only 182 out of 3,068 were sent to prison for drunken driving, and for cases of reckless or dangerous driving it was 116 out of 4,584. She compared this for the offence of begging, where out of 590 adults convicted, 236 were sent to prison. All this led her to give support to the Marxist theory that the law is made and operated for the well-to-do.

Thirdly, there were the explanations offered for the motoring offender. She found these deficient. She spells this out in one paragraph of her paper entitled 'Who Are the Criminals?'[14] First she points to the criminologists themselves. In studies of geographical areas in which offenders live, she said criminologists habitually omit motoring crimes from their study. Second, the situation was made worse by the then-practice of having motoring offenders dealt with in separate courts, giving the impression of a qualitatively different type of offence and offender. Third, when motoring offenders were eventually convicted, they were again treated as a separate category of offenders when their previous convictions were not listed to the court.

Bringing attention to the position (or plight) of the motoring offender at a time when motoring offences were often not seen as crimes was striking. Over the years, that view has changed, especially over drunken driving, where the offender has less sympathy. Yet Barbara Wootton was one of the few criminologists to emphasise the point that motoring offences were crimes, and that the police were not 'wasting their time catching motorists when they should be catching real criminals'.

Yet having challenged conventional attitudes, what then? Was Barbara Wootton asking for more motoring offenders to be sentenced to imprisonment or asking for more nonmotoring offenders to be given less severe sentences? It is not clear. And what of the range of sentences offered? She makes no comment on the way courts rarely ask for a social enquiry report on a motoring offender or rarely if ever make a probation order for certain motoring offences.[15]

Generally speaking, the sociodemographics of offenders have remained roughly the same in the following decades, but the patterns of criminality have changed enormously. The peak age of crime (reported offences and cleared up) has hardly changed, there are still more male offenders than female, and motoring offenders still dominate court lists. Yet much else has changed, making today's lists almost unrecognisable from those of the early 1960s. An obvious change has been in the use of drugs and its associated criminality. Few drug users appeared before the courts in the 1960s, and the professional drug dealer was unknown – so too with cybercrime, again unknown in the 1960s. Levels of female violence have also increased. Whether Barbara Wootton as magistrate would recognise the current court list is difficult to say. She might be dismayed at the background of some offenders and their failings socially and educationally. For example, she would be concerned about the numbers of young men aged 30 years or less appearing before her who have never been in employment, have poor levels of literacy and present multiple problems.

Cannabis Report

I have included the Cannabis Report within the context of this chapter. It was aimed at recasting the drug legislation, amending the existing law relating to cannabis and reviewing police powers of search and arrest in relation to drug offences generally. Its main conclusion was as stated by the Chairman of the Advisory Committee on Drug Dependence, namely that the Report was a plea for the use of cannabis to be judged more realistically in the light of existing knowledge and pending further research. As such, it was concerned primarily with the legal processes as they existed then and in the future.

In 1968, a subcommittee of the Advisory Committee on Drug Dependence, of which Barbara Wootton was a member, was asked 'to review available evidence on the pharmacological, clinical, pathological, social and legal aspects of these drugs'. Or more specifically, it was the Hallucinogens Sub Committee, as the Committee was asked to include LSD (Lysergic Acid Diethylamide), but it concentrated on cannabis. Barbara Wootton was asked to chair this subcommittee; hence the Report was hereafter referred to as the Wootton Report. A second Report on LSD and amphetamines came later.

The background and debates on the Cannabis Report are interesting. They show how the Report was received by government initially and the impact and influence it had on government policy in Britain over the following decades. New forms of drug use were producing a typical moral panic with all its attendant hallmarks; for example, there were demands for increased penalties, for heavier sentences for the pusher – who were seen to differ from the user and were more culpable – for more police enforcement and for a less sympathetic approach to drug users generally. Cannabis was singled out for special attention; it was seen as a 'gateway' drug, leading from the soft to the hard, in this case from cannabis to heroin. The problem centred around that group of users called 'addicts', i.e., almost exclusively addicted to heroin, often taken with cocaine. Cannabis was also considered a dangerous drug, producing psychotic episodes among its users, but not considered as dangerous as heroin.

The background to the Wootton report goes back some 10 years when, in 1959, an Interdepartmental Committee under the chairmanship of Lord Brain was appointed with terms of reference 'to review in the light of recent developments advice given to an earlier Committee on morphine and heroin addiction'.[16] It reported in 1961. It was not clear what those 'recent developments' were, but it was suspected that they related to an increase in heroin use largely due to overprescribing by a small number of doctors. (The so-called British system permitted any qualified medical practitioner to prescribe to addicts for medical treatment any controlled substance, including heroin or cannabis – the term 'medical treatment' to be interpreted widely.) In 1953, there were 290 heroin addicts in Britain, which had increased to 454 in 1959, an increase of 89%. The increase was thought to be related entirely to a group of young, male, nontherapeutic addicts who took drugs for pleasure, i.e., as opposed to the so-called therapeutic addicts who were prescribed the drugs for the relief of pain, invariably due to a terminal condition. This new group were thought to be overprescribed. There had also been an increase in the use of cannabis, but no figures were available. A number of jazz musicians in Soho were known to have been smoking cannabis, and it was thought that these musicians were setting a new and growing trend. However, in spite of these fears, the first Brain Committee believed no new controls were necessary as addiction to all dangerous drugs 'was still very small'. Such increases as existed were thought to be an 'extension to addiction', and the Committee thought this related to 'an intensified activity for its detection'. No further action was required.

However, by 1964, conditions had deteriorated. The number of known addicts increased to 753, with predictions that there would be 11,000 by 1972, and one journalist thought there would be 1 million new addicts created in 1984 for that year alone. The Brain Committee was hastily reconvened. It saw the problem as being created by 'the activities of a very few doctors who have prescribed excessively for addicts'. In a now-famous passage, the Committee said it was informed that 'in 1962 one doctor alone prescribed almost 6 kgms for addicts (which was one-sixth of all the heroin produced in Britain in 1962) and 2 doctors each issued a single prescription for 1,000 tablets'. (Barbara Wootton in a different context said the problem was not that of one or two overprescribing doctors, but of the many who prescribed more than was required.) The Committee thought that the problem was one of control: if there was insufficient control, that might lead to a further spread of addiction; if restrictions were too severe, that might prevent or seriously discourage the addict from obtaining drugs legitimately – in which case the addict might resort to acquiring them illegitimately, which would lead to further growth in organised traffic. The second Brain Committee's solution was to introduce treatment centres whereby these centres could permit doctors to prescribe heroin for this group of addicts. There were also fears that cannabis use alongside other drugs was on the rise, and that cannabis was leading to the use of more serious drugs.

Most of the changes proposed by the second Brain Committee were accepted by the government, but not that which suggested the treatment centres should have powers to detain an addict during a crisis in treatment. The Brain Committee had said there was 'the obstinacy of some addicts and the likelihood that they will break off their treatment' – a wise move. This was rightly interpreted as being a recommendation for the compulsory detention of drug users.

The 1960s was of course also the time of the so called permissive society. Drugs, and especially cannabis, were seen as in the forefront of permissiveness, creating and fostering new ways of behaving which challenged traditional views. There was much talk among the drug-using community of the value and importance of extrasensory perception and having numerous other intrapsychic experiences. They spoke of new levels of consciousness and of heightening sensual and mystical experience. Aldous Huxley's book *The Doors of Perception* was said to offer important insights into this new world – although how many actually read it is not known. Of course, the term 'permissive' extended to areas other than drug-taking, but drugs, drug use and the supposed attendant criminality were seen as exemplars of permissiveness. The term 'permissive society' became pejorative, although Barbara Wootton thought otherwise, believing it denoted a welcome change towards an decrease in controls, and she wondered how society can be permissive as long as the law remains that it is an offence to possess cannabis, just as it is an offence to be drunk and disorderly.[17] She thought too there was no need to panic; drugs 'were the mode of the moment' and a way of making life more tolerable. They were also a means of rebellion.

> Partly I think the younger generation like to take cannabis for very much the same reasons as younger women now use eye shadow instead of lipstick, – because their mothers use lipstick they have to use eye shadow and no lipstick.[18]

If she thought drug use was a simple rebellion likely to last for a short time to be replaced by another mode of fashion, she misunderstood its nature and impact.

Nonetheless, it is against this background that the Cannabis Report was produced. It was presented to the Home Secretary, James Callaghan, on 1 November 1968, at the height of the 1960s period of permissiveness. It is a carefully argued report, dealing with a number of issues, not just about the drug itself or about its links with criminality, although these are dealt with, but about wider questions which continue to dominate the debate, albeit some 50 years later. The most notable of these concerns the question whether it is justifiable for the law to restrict a man's freedom in what is presumed to be in his own interest. The Sub Committee referred to John Stuart Mill's famous dictum that 'the only purpose for which power can rightly be exercised over any member of a civilised community against his will is to prevent harm to others. His own good either physical or moral is not a sufficient warrant.'

The Sub Committee tackled this head on. Drug-taking, it said, can be seen as a self-regarding act, and if so, it is not the law's business to interfere with a person's actions even if those actions may be seen as damaging to that person's interests. If the person is an adult (the J.S. Mill dictum does not apply to children or those not in the maturity of their actions) and wishes to take a drug which may ultimately harm him, then so be it. That is his decision; adults ought to be free to decide according to personal tastes and their own moral judgements how best they should proceed. If that means taking substances which others consider harmful or morally unacceptable, then that is an individual decision. The Sub Committee pointed out that such an argument was used by the Wolfenden Committee in 1957 when considering homosexuality, and which Parliament accepted, that homosexual acts committed in private between consenting adults ought not be the subject of criminal proceedings. It also pointed out that suicide attempts are not criminal, and anyone over a certain age is entitled to ride a motorcycle although the statistics of self-destruction bear eloquent testimony to the lethal character of these machines.[19] It is an argument still used by those wishing to legalise drugs, suggesting in the same terms as John Stuart Mill that drug-taking is 'not the laws business'.[20]

On the other hand, the Sub Committee recognised that drug-taking generally, and cannabis use in particular, was not a wholly self-regarding act. Indeed, few acts are. The Sub Committee said cannabis use is other-regarding in that its use involves wider social consequences including its effects on immediate families. Accordingly, the Sub Committee said 'every proposal to restrict freedom of the individual in his own supposed interest must therefore be decided on its merits.'[21] In saying this, the Committee avoided a discussion as to why cannabis was other-regarding and alcohol or tobacco not. It also said there was the problem of public attitudes, although it is not clear what they meant by this. They said too, and with some prescience, that laws which seek to control the personal consumption of individuals are notoriously difficult to enforce – and could have added that they evoke considerable antagonism towards the agents of law enforcement as occurs with the stop-and-search procedures.

The Sub Committee's conclusion was that, on the evidence they received, and much of it was contradictory, cannabis was a dangerous drug, but in terms of physical harmfulness was not as dangerous as opiates, barbiturates or amphetamines.[22]

> We conclude therefore in the interests of public health it is necessary to maintain restrictions on the availability and use of this drug. For the purpose of enforcing these restrictions there is no alternative to the criminal law and its penalties.[23]

As for cannabis being a gateway drug, the Sub Committee concluded that on the evidence they obtained it was clear that many heroin addicts had previously sampled cannabis before taking heroin, but they had also sampled other drugs as well. The Sub Committee said that those using cannabis were more likely than those who were not using it to take heroin, but it was the personality of the user rather than the properties of the drug that was likely to cause progressions.[24]

And the links with crime? Again, the Sub Committee said the evidence was not forthcoming. An excessive dose of cannabis may lead to an attack of disturbed consciousness, excitement, agitation, panic or reduced self-control, but the extent to which this leads a person to commit violent crime, said the Sub Committee, depends more on the offender than on the drug.[25] It was recognised that a number of criminals take cannabis but so do others, and it was not possible, given the methods of detecting cannabis in the body, to talk of a direct link.

The Sub Committee having decided that cannabis should be a controlled drug, what of the penalties? In a key paragraph, the Sub Committee said, 'We believe that the association with heroin and the other opiates is entirely inappropriate and that new and quite separate legislation to deal specially and separately with cannabis and its synthetic derivatives should be introduced as soon as possible.' And in the same paragraph, 'We are also convinced that the present penalties for possession and supply are altogether too high.'[26] The Sub Committee proposed a distinction to be made between possession of small amounts for personal use and possession with intent to supply.

The Report also proposed a number of changes to existing penalties. The main ones were to suggest that on summary conviction there would be a fine of a maximum of £200.00, and on indictment the fine would be unlimited or a sentence not exceeding two years or both. The maximum penalty for smuggling cannabis was to be reduced to two years. These proposals would reduce existing penalties and were consistent with the approach that cannabis needed to be controlled, but it was not as dangerous as the opiates where the suggested penalties were higher.

The Report was greeted with approval in some quarters, dismay in others. Home Secretary James Callaghan said he would reject the Report. He told Parliament that the Committee had been overinfluenced by the legalisation lobby. He said 'it was wrong for the committee to report on one drug in isolation in the way that it did.' He also said that

> I think it came as a surprise if not a shock to most people to find that there was a lobby in favour of legalising cannabis. My reading of that Report is that the Wootton Sub Committee was over influenced by this lobby. I had the impression that those that were in favour of legalising 'pot' were all the time pushing the other members of the Committee back.

This produced a vigorous response from Barbara Wootton and the Chairman of the Advisory Committee, Sir Edward Wayne. In a letter to *The Times* (5 February 1969), they said,

> We regard this statement as offensive to our distinguished colleagues and ourselves and particularly to the eminent medical men who signed our Report, and we particularly deprecate the implications of the emotive word 'lobby' in this context. We would also point out that after hearing the evidence no member of the Sub Committee recommended legalisation.

However, a year later the Home Secretary introduced comprehensive new consolidating legislation that had the effect of implementing Barbara Wootton's proposals.

Barbara Wootton's own reaction to what she called 'this hysteria' which she thought came a great deal from the press, from a considerable part of the public, and apart from one or two outstanding exceptions, from a number of MPs, was put it down to a situation where 'some critical or objective study threatens to block an outlet for indulgence in the pleasures of moral indignation.' Even so, she thought it a matter of grave concern that young people take drugs without knowledge of the consequences, but she did not think this was a subject for hysteria.[27]

There are a number of points from the Cannabis Report that require emphasis. First, the Sub Committee aired the John Stuart Mill argument about negative liberty, and although the committee concluded that this did not apply in the use of cannabis – the use of cannabis was not a wholly self-regarding act – the argument needed to be stated. Second, cannabis might be dangerous, but it was not as dangerous as drugs such as the opiates. Third, cannabis was not a gateway drug. Fourth, cannabis did not lead to crime, although of course some offenders smoked cannabis. Fifth, the penalties for cannabis were too high; and finally a distinction in law should be made between possession for personal use and possession with intent to supply. Given the febrile atmosphere at the time – the Home Secretary's response is an example – and a less considered report, one given over to some of the more extreme demands, British drug legislation would likely have taken a different and more extreme form. This would not have been to anyone's advantage: the public, law enforcement or the drug users. We could have easily slipped into a period whereby lengthy prison sentences would be the norm, with an excessive cost to the taxpayer and little benefit to anyone else. It is not, of course, possible to assess the impact of the Cannabis Report on government or society generally. It may be that the government would have arrived at similar conclusions irrespective of the Wootton Report, but doubtful. A legacy of the Wootton Report was its tolerance of a problem that was viewed by many as out of control.

Another legacy of the Cannabis Report was the consideration given to the question of the police powers of 'stop and search'. The Sub Committee (paragraph 10) recommended that the Advisory Committee should undertake as a matter of urgency a review of police powers of stop and search in relation to drug offences generally. A member of that Committee, Michael Schofield, put the matter more strongly. He thought powers of stop and search were already too wide. Existing powers allow the police to stop and search

> without warrant any person reasonably suspected of being in unlawful possession of drugs. The dangers in these powers are immense, for there is only the subjective word 'reasonably' to prevent the over zealous from stopping and searching anyone for anything anywhere.[28]

It is a problem still with us: increase powers of stop and search and there will be an increase in convictions but a decrease in civil liberties; reduce powers of stop and search and the converse occurs. Finding an appropriate balance seems more or less impossible.

Noncustodial sentences: the Community Service Order

It was the Report on 'Non-custodial and semi-custodial penalties' whereby Barbara Wootton made another of her important contributions to criminology and penal policy.[29] This Report came two years after the Cannabis Report. It arose in strangely similar circumstances insofar as the then–Home Secretary Roy Jenkins asked the Advisory Council on the Penal System to consider what changes and additions might be made to the existing range of noncustodial penalties. The Council again appointed a subcommittee under the chairmanship of Barbara Wootton. It reported on June 1970. The Report itself was another triumph; it was well written, concise and well argued. This time it was also well received, quite different from the visceral accusations surrounding 'Cannabis'.

The Report dealt with a range of noncustodial penalties, including the so-called day fine, the deferred sentence, junior and senior attendance centres and the use of disqualification and forfeiture. However, its main recommendation and claim to posterity was the proposal for a Community Service Order. This was an order for 'unpaid community service as a new form of non custodial sentence'. The Advisory Council called it 'imaginative and hopeful'. Similar sentiments were expressed by the then-government. Within two years, many of the proposals had been introduced into the 1972 Criminal Justice Act with only three minor modifications. First, the number of hours of community service recommended by the Report was 120, to be completed within six months. The Act doubled this and also imposed a minimum of 40 hours. Second, the Community Service Order (CSO) was to be a sentence of the court and not a condition of a probation order (a probation order was not a sentence; the offender had to agree to be placed on probation). Finally, the Act limited the application of CSOs to persons convicted of imprisonment, whereas the Report would have cast its net wider to catch certain types of traffic offenders – an obvious example of Barbara Wootton's influence and a continuation of her wish to cast traffic offenders within the same provisions as for other criminals.

The background to the Report was such that something needed to be done about a high and increasing prison population, with poor success rates and overcramped conditions. There was also the belief that short-term prison sentences were not producing satisfactory results; short-term sentences were seen as disruptive rather than rehabilitative, and associated with high reconviction rates. A community sentence was required, which was more punitive than probation and filled the gap between custodial and noncustodial sentences. CSOs appeared to do just that.

Apparently, according to her biographer Ann Oakley, the idea for the CSO was Barbara's. Her biographer describes how the idea 'floated' into her mind one day on the common-sense basis that instead of sending offenders to prison it would be better to get them to do some useful work.[30] Other members of the Sub Committee eagerly agreed with the suggestion. However, Norval Morris and Michael Tonry take a different view. They see the origins of community service as somewhere back in the 17th century, where offenders were press ganged into the British Navy. They trace its modern version to Alameda County, California, USA in 1966, where it was used as a punishment for traffic offenders, usually imposed as a condition of probation. Whatever the origins, Morris and Tonry alongside their British counterparts all agree that in its modern resurgence, the CSO is one of the more promising intermediate punishments in a rational punishment system.[31]

It was always said that the strength of the CSO proposal was its appeal to different penal philosophies – a strength which Barbara Wootton trumpeted but said she felt slightly ashamed of, as it was an undisguised attempt at currying favour.[32] First, the CSO was retributive; the punishment would fit the crime. Second, it was a deterrent to the individual offender and to the community. Thirdly, it was rehabilitative in that the offenders might learn values and practices that would lead them away from crime. Finally, it was reparative in that the offender paid back something to the community for the wrong he had committed. Of course, over and above these penal philosophies, there were pragmatic aims: to reduce levels of incarceration by providing an alternative to prison, and to reduce offending. In doing so, it offered a certain appeal to the courts and others. Barbara Wootton thought acceptance by the probation service was also essential, as the probation service would be responsible for arranging the work and supervising the programme.[33] The probation service, however, was initially hostile, seeing the CSO as in competition with the probation order and bringing a more punitive stance to community penalties.

The American Bar Association defines community service thus: 'A community service programme is a programme through which convicted offenders are placed in unpaid positions with non profit or tax supported agencies to serve a specified number of hours performing work or service within a given time limit as a sentencing option or condition.'[34] This definition encapsulates many of the key features of a CSO. Offenders are not paid; this in part is to avoid accusations of the chain gang approach, but also to avoid the displacement of free labour, i.e., competing for the work of nonoffenders. The type of work suitable for CSOs was seen as likely to be community service programmes such as those in homes for the aged, in mental hospitals, or typically other work undertaken by volunteers. Included in the previously given definition are the time limits imposed in the Order, which started at 240 hours but have since increased. What is not included in the American Bar Association definition but is in the Court Order in Britain are the arrangements for supervision and breach proceedings if the offender breaks the conditions of his Order. Also not included are age and work restrictions: an offender must be over the age of 16 years and suitable for work, and such work must be available. In Britain, a CSO is a standalone sentence, whereas elsewhere, such as in the USA, it is often part of another order, usually a probation order.

In 1972, Parliament accepted the recommendations of the Sub Committee, and in 1973 six probation areas were selected in England and Wales as 'experimental' areas. The first CSO was said to have been made in Nottingham on 2 January 1973, but this is disputed by Ken Pease and Bill McWilliams, who say it was first made in Bow Street Magistrates Court for possession of cannabis, and the sentence was passed by Sir Frank Milton, the Chief Metropolitan Stipendiary Magistrate.[35] In 1975, the CSO programme was extended to other probation areas. If measured in terms of popularity, CSOs were an undoubted success; in the following year, 1976, the number of orders imposed reached 9,133, nearly three times the figure for the previous year. Barbara Wootton, writing for *The Probation Journal* in 1977, was clearly pleased with the way CSOs had been accepted, saying 'Community Service has caught on better than I dared to hope.'[36] She was correct to say the popularity of the CSO depended on the Probation Service, which was likely to determine the future of the scheme. It was the Probation Service who by its recommendation in Social Enquiry Reports determined its overall use and after its initial hostility had slowly begun to accept it. Nevertheless, fashions in sentencing come and go,[37] although in this case CSOs seemed to have remained popular.

Like all sentences, CSOs must find their place on the tariff, and in doing so draw from those above who would have been given a more severe sentence, probably imprisonment, and those below who would have been given a sentence less severe, probably a fine or probation order. In all new sentences, there is an element of 'net widening', and the CSO is no exception: 'net widening' in this case occurring when those below are dragged into a higher tariff sentence than would have occurred otherwise. How many offenders on CSOs would have otherwise been sentenced to a lower tariff sentence is impossible to say, as is the opposite, i.e., how many would have been sent to prison. The hope has always been that CSOs have produced a reduction in the prison population. Whether true or not, the failure rate, measured by reconvictions, has been noticeably high, or rather higher than expected. An evaluation of CSO cases in June 1977 showed that 44.2% were reconvicted within one year, against

33.3% of a control group which had been recommended by the probation service for a CSO but had been otherwise dealt with. These results should be treated with caution, however, not only for the weakness of the control group but because the evaluation covered only the six pilot areas, and it came before little experience had been gained as the selection of cases.[38] Nonetheless, whichever way one looks at it, the results were mediocre at best.

Barbara Wootton said whatever the reconviction rate, a CSO was still cheaper than prison, a point incidentally often made by probation officers about the probation order. But the matter is not quite that simple. The expected savings on so-called gaol time, i.e., from fewer offenders sent to prison, turn out to be difficult to calculate, or if not then somewhat illusory. Savings only become relevant when large numbers of offenders are kept out of prison, and/or when no new prisons are built, and/or no new prison wings are needed, and/or no extra staff are required. Only then can we reasonably talk of savings. And these have to be offset by the likelihood that courts might send more offenders to prison, and for longer periods, knowing there are more prison places. Then there is the 'net widening' factor to be considered, i.e., those who would have received a less severe sentence being pulled into a higher tariff sentence. All these factors neutralise otherwise benefits.

There is, however, a positive side, which is the financial contribution made to the community. Morris and Tonry say it is difficult, almost impossible, to calculate the extent of savings in terms of the value to community service programmes, although Joan Petersilia in 1987 calculated that the New York City programme produced a total contribution that year for the 7,500 offenders of about $2.5 million.[39] Morris and Tonry thought that there was an additional hidden value in the services performed under CSOs in that the work undertaken tends to be greatly appreciated by those who are its recipients, i.e., living in the community.

An unexpected failing – at least unexpected by Barbara Wootton – has been the inconsistent supervision of the CSOs. This largely surrounds offenders' attendance, or rather the lack of it, and inconsistencies come from corresponding decisions to breach. This is not just a problem for CSOs but has been a problem with all community-based orders, whether they be probation orders, supervision orders, combination orders or the like. Various attempts have been made to produce a solution, one of which has been to rename the CSO a Community Punishment Order, a change that Barbara Wootton would not have welcomed. Another has been to introduce National Standards. These were first introduced in 1969 for all community-based orders and further revised and toughened in 2000. Carol Hedderman and Mike Hough say as a result there are now few circumstances in which an absence may be regarded as acceptable and virtually every case in which more than one unacceptable absence occurs will go to court for breach proceedings.[40] The Criminal Justice Act 2003 further provided a statutory duty for the responsible officer to institute breach proceedings if there is an unacceptable failure within 12 months. Again, it is not clear how Barbara Wootton would have reacted to these changes; she may have seen them as too punitive for her liking. The probation service certainly thought so.

However, an unexpected but interesting development – again unexpected by Barbara Wootton – has been about supervision and the conditions of the orders. This has led to a debate about the nature of supervision and the legal controls imposed on offenders in the community. What rules are required, and what should be the levels of enforcement? Questions about the nature of rules suggest they become troublesome, to use one of David Faulkner's terms, when they make demands which are beyond the offender's capacity to cope. Rules should be sufficient to ensure the offender moves into a settled way of life and not add to the punishment already inflicted. An impact of stricter levels of enforcement have produced some troubling results and, paradoxically, sometimes produced more criminality. Take for example parole supervision, where an increasingly large number are recalled to prison, not for committing further offences but for noncompliance with parole requirements. The figures up to 31 March 2017 for England and Wales show that 47% of offenders on parole were recalled for noncompliance, a number so large as to make up a significant proportion of the prison population. The fear is that we may be following the American pattern, where an increase in the prison population comes not from immediate offences but failing to meet the conditions of a community order. Already we have, under Section 8 of the Criminal Justice Act 2003, powers to imprison offenders for breaches of a Community Order, even when the original offence was not punishable by imprisonment. I doubt if these developments would have pleased Barbara Wootton, but they have been some of the unexpected consequences of her proposals.[41]

The Report on Non Custodial Sentences involved more than CSOs, but included *inter alia* a discussion on day fines. I mention these briefly as they reflect a typical Wootton-type view of sentencing, and one can see why she found the day fine attractive. The day fine was introduced in Sweden in 1932 in order that monetary penalties for criminal offences should affect the rich and poor more equitably. It works on the basis of multiplying a number accorded to the seriousness of the offence with the offender's ability to pay. Never mind the difficulties of enforcement in Britain, where information on the offender's means is more difficult to obtain than in Sweden; the direction of the sentence is clearly towards the offender rather than the offence. The Committee on Non Custodial Penalties thought that 'fines should be assessed according to the offender's ability to pay', adding that 'in our view it is right that penalties for similar offences should as far as possible be designed to make an equal impact on offenders, and that the well to do should pay more than the less affluent.'[42] One can hear Barbara Wootton's voice in every line of this paragraph of the Report, with it ending on 'The fine will be more equitable only if it is assessed in this way and constitutes something more than payment for a licence to commit the particular offence.'[43]

The day fine system, which is directed towards the offender rather than the offence, was certainly not in accordance with the tariff. It was tried in Britain but abandoned due to the difficulty of enforcement, and the way in which someone who was well to do paid an enormous fine for a relatively minor offence. Objections were that the day fine was not in accordance with justice (read the tariff), but of course justice was not foremost in Barbara Wootton's thinking.

The Report on Non Custodial Penalties contained proposals for numerous other sentences, including the deferred sentence, disqualification and forfeiture, weekend imprisonment and attendance centres. The Sub Committee thought there was a strong case for introducing a deferred sentence along the lines of that existing in Scotland whereby a court can defer a sentence to provide an opportunity for an offender to show good behaviour, repay money he has acquired dishonestly, pay compensation for damage for which he has caused maliciously, or to perform some other act which would indicate the ability to stay out of trouble.[44]

The proposals on disqualification and forfeiture are interesting in that some have been introduced in subsequent legislation, albeit in modified forms; others not. The question of depriving an offender the proceeds of his crime was dealt with by another Sub Committee and in the field of drug offences has had considerable impact. The Wootton Sub Committee dealt with other matters, one of which remains of contemporary interest: the employment of persons with criminal convictions who work in certain occupations, for example the employment of offenders with convictions for sex offences working with children. The Wootton Committee thought there was a case for a statutory provision which would enable courts, when persons are found guilty of certain offences, to make orders prohibiting them from taking certain kinds of employment.[45]

Proposals not included in legislation are those involving the offender losing his driving licence over weekends and being sentenced to weekend imprisonment. Both sentences were said by the Committee to be attractive proposals, and the government was urged in both cases to give them serious consideration. Both plainly demonstrate the Wootton influence. There were similar arguments for each proposal, namely that they avoid loss of earnings and loss of occupation. The Committee thought that the loss of one's driving licence has several undesirable side effects, one of which is if the offender has a job he is likely to lose it. So, the proposal was that offenders who were disqualified from driving would lose their licences only over weekends. Losing one's licence only over weekends would provide the necessary punishment. The argument was the same for weekend imprisonment, which the Sub Committee called 'Intermittent Custody'; again the Committee said offenders would be less likely to lose their job if incarcerated on weekends, although the case for weekend imprisonment was stronger in that if living with a wife and family, the offender is compulsorily removed from them with all the consequences that may involve.[46] Neither proposal was accepted; practical problems and the costs involved in administering the programmes were deciding factors.

An interesting outcome of the debate on CSOs concerned the role and input of the press, including TV, and of the role and influence of the TV presenter. It started as a debate about statistics: first about the reconviction rates of those on CSOs, where it was suggested these offenders had a higher reconviction rate than those in the control group. Barbara Wootton challenged these figures; she said they were not chosen on randomly selected control groups, but on 'dubious comparability' between the groups. The BBC said it was 'statistical fact' that offenders given CSOs were as likely as exprisoners to reoffend. In a different programme, the BBC kept this 'fact' in because the programme makers had talked to a number of probation officers who said CSOs did not work. Again, Barbara Wootton challenged this, but by careful manipulation the programme cut up Barbara Wootton's interview, resulting in passages acquiring entirely different meanings. Her letter to *The Times* (February 1966) sparked off a debate about the distortions programme makers could engineer, thereby creating different impressions which suit their views and opinions.[47]

This Sub Committee Report has had an impact on the development and growth of noncustodial sentences in England and Wales, and for many countries besides. It helped fill the gap between imprisonment and probation, described by Norval Morris and Michael Tonry, where 'between the two is a near vacuum of purposive and enforced punishments. Too many are in prison and too few have enforced control in the community.'[48] The Report was another triumph for Barbara Wootton and increased her standing in the community. The Criminal Justice Act 1972 contains the Wootton proposals, such as the deferred sentence in Section 22, forfeiture of property in Section 23 and the CSO in Section 15. Barbara was particularly proud of the CSO proposal, telling a journalist, 'This is about the only thing I've got written down in the book I'm going to show St Peter when I get there.' As her biographer said, she had a lot more to show than that.[49]

Conclusion

Barbara Wootton's criminological interests covered a wide area, and her influence was such as to include many different aspects of contemporary criminology. Perhaps her most notable achievements came from those two Sub Committee Reports, on cannabis and noncustodial penalties, both of which had a lasting impact on law and jurisprudence: one, on legal approaches to a serious social problem, the other on the development of legal penalties within the community.

The two Reports were perhaps Barbara Wootton's most notable achievements, at least in terms of introducing legislation which had a lasting impact. The first Report did much to temper a debate which was bordering on hysterical, and help set the scene for a more rational drug policy. One could imagine how a less considered Report could have led to a more intensive reaction, and to more-intensive consequences. The Home Secretary's response to the Report says it all. And he was not alone. Numerous other MPs reacted in a similar way. Of course it was not just a Report by Barbara Wootton; others contributed, but as she chaired the Committee, Barbara Wootton had major influence, and it was from the outset known as the 'Wootton Report'. The style and content was evidence of her influence.

The Report on Non Custodial Penalties was different. It introduced a new sentence for the courts and helped fill the gap in the available sentences in the community. It has long been recognised that existing sentences such as the fine, conditional discharge and probation order were not sufficiently punitive or demanding, and something else was required. The CSO appeared to offer that provision. That it was presented in a way which unashamedly appealed to almost every interested party, and satisfied almost every theory of punishment, was to its advantage. Few proposals begin with such universal appeal.

Barbara Wootton's contribution to other aspects of the criminological spectrum was more limited. She had little to say that was new in her examination of the criminal statistics, although she drew attention to the anomalies and special privileges which seem to be attached to the motoring offender. Given the spirit of the times, it was a significant contribution. Her comments still remain relevant some six decades later; there is still a reluctance to see the motoring offender as a criminal, although perhaps less so for the drunken driver, but even here, as with the middle-class cocaine user, different explanations are offered for the criminality – stress at work, etc. To Barbara Wootton's credit, she would have none of that.

Notes

1 Home Office (1968) *Cannabis. Report by the Advisory Committee on Drug Dependence*. HMSO.
2 Home Office (1970) *Non Custodial and Semi Custodial Penalties. Report of the Advisory Council on the Penal System*. HMSO.
3 Fyval T. (1963) *The Insecure Offenders Penguin*. This was one of the most influential at the time.
4 Wootton B (1959) *Social Science and Social Pathology*. George Allen and Unwin p. 193.
5 Wootton B (1963) *Crime and the Criminal Law: Reflections of a Magistrate and a Social Scientist*. (The Hamlyn Lectures) Stevens and Sons. (Second Edition 1981 with postscripts to each chapter) p. 5 and Wootton B (1959) *Social Science and Social Pathology*. George Allen and Unwin. op. cit. pp. 30–31.
6 Wootton B (1959) *Social Science and Social Pathology*. George Allen and Unwin. op. cit. p. 318.
7 Wootton B (1963) *Crime and the Criminal Law: Reflections of a Magistrate and a Social Scientist*. (The Hamlyn Lectures) Stevens and Sons. (Second Edition 1981 with postscripts to each chapter). op. cit. p. 8.
8 Ibid. p. 7.
9 Wootton B (1967) *In a World I Never Made. Autobiographical Reflections*. George Allen and Unwin p. 160.
10 Wootton B (1963) *Crime and the Criminal Law: Reflections of a Magistrate and a Social Scientist*. (The Hamlyn Lectures) Stevens and Sons. (Second Edition 1981 with postscripts to each chapter). op. cit. A slightly different version is found in Barbara Wootton Selected Writings Vol. 1 Crime and the penal system p. 6.
11 Wootton B (1975/1992) Who are the criminals? Reprinted In Seal V and Bean P (eds) *Barbara Wootton Selected Writings Vol. 1 Crime and the Penal System* pp. 109–117.
12 Ibid. p. 116.
13 Ibid. p. 111.
14 Ibid. p. 113.

15 Incidentally, one wonders too how many motoring offenders were sent to prison, or probation reports requested with Baroness Wootton of Abinger as Chairman of the Bench. She doesn't say!
16 Most of this debate is taken from Bean PT (1974) *The Social Control of Drugs*. Martin Robertson.
17 Wootton B (1975/1992) Time and the drug scene. Reprinted In Seal V and Bean P (eds) *Barbara Wootton Selected Writings Vol. 1 Crime and the Penal System* p 136.
18 Ibid. p. 136.
19 Home Office (1968) *Cannabis. Report by the Advisory Committee on Drug Dependence*. HMSO. op. cit. para 15.
20 See Bean PT (2009) *Legalising Drugs*. Policy Press.
21 Home Office (1968) *Cannabis. Report by the Advisory Committee on Drug Dependence*. HMSO. op. cit. para 16.
22 Ibid. para 70.
23 Ibid. para 71.
24 Ibid. paras 48–51.
25 Ibid. para 55.
26 Ibid. para 81.
27 House of Lords Debates. Hansard 20 March 1969 cols. 1305–1314.
28 Home Office (1968) *Cannabis. Report by the Advisory Committee on Drug Dependence*. HMSO. op. cit. para 11.
29 Home Office (1970) *Non Custodial and Semi Custodial Penalties. Report of the Advisory Council on the Penal System*. HMSO. op. cit.
30 Oakley A (2011) *A Critical Woman*. Bloomsbury Academic p. 272.
31 Morris N and Tonry M (1990) *Between Prison and Probation*. Oxford University Press p. 152.
32 Wootton B (1978) *Crime and Penal Policy; Reflections on Fifty Years Experience*. Allen and Unwin p. 128.
33 See also para 33 of the Non Custodial and Semi Custodial Penalties Report.
34 Quoted in Morris N and Tonry M (1990) *Between Prison and Probation*. Oxford University Press. op. cit. p. 152.
35 Pease K and McWilliams W (1980) *Community Service by Order*. Scottish Academic Press. p. 31.
36 Wootton B. (1975/1992) Some reflections on the first five years of community service. Reprinted In Seal V and Bean P (eds) *Barbara Wootton Selected Writings Vol. 1 Crime and the Penal System* p. 143.
37 Ibid. p. 145.
38 Ibid.
39 Morris N and Tonry M (1990) *Between Prison and Probation*. Oxford University Press. op. cit. p. 156.
40 Hedderman C and Hough M (2004) Getting tough or being effective. In Mair G (ed) *What Matters in Probation*. Willan p. 152.
41 Webster R (2017) *Why Are Offenders Recalled to Prison?* Online at russellwebser.com (19 October).
42 Home Office (1970) *Non Custodial and Semi Custodial Penalties. Report of the Advisory Council on the Penal System*. HMSO. op. cit. para 18.
43 Ibid.

44 Ibid. para 81.
45 Ibid. para 136.
46 Ibid. para 151.
47 Oakley A (2011) A *Critical Woman*. Bloomsbury Academic. op. cit. p. 274.
48 Morris N and Tonry M (1990) *Between Prison and Probation*. Oxford University Press. op. cit. p. 3.
49 Oakley A (2011) A *Critical Woman*. Bloomsbury Academic. op. cit. p. 276.

References for publications by Barbara Wootton

Wootton B (1950) *Testament for Social Science*. George Allen and Unwin.

Wootton B (1959) *Social Science and Social Pathology*. George Allen and Unwin.

Wootton B (1962) A *Social Scientists Approach to Maternal Deprivation in Deprivation of Maternal Care; A Reassessment of Its Effects*. WHO pp. 63–73.

Wootton B (1963) *Crime and the Criminal Law: Reflections of a Magistrate and a Social Scientist* (The Hamlyn Lectures) Stevens and Sons. (Second Edition 1981 with postscripts to each chapter).

Wootton B (1967) *In a World I Never Made. Autobiographical Reflections*. George Allen and Unwin.

Wootton B (1975) The administration of justice. Lecture given to the University of Leeds. Reprinted In Seal V and Bean P (eds) *Barbara Wootton Selected Writings Vol. 1 Crime and the Penal System* pp. 95–108.

Wootton B. (1975) Some reflections on the first five years of community service. Reprinted In Seal V and Bean P (eds) *Barbara Wootton Selected Writings Vol. 1 Crime and the Penal System* pp. 143–145.

Wootton B (1975) Who are the criminals? Reprinted In Seal V and Bean P (eds) *Barbara Wootton Selected Writings Vol. 1 Crime and the Penal System* pp. 109–117.

Wootton B (1975) Time and the drug scene. Reprinted In Seal V and Bean P (eds) *Barbara Wootton Selected Writings Vol. 1 Crime and the Penal System* pp. 135–137.

Wootton B (1978) *Crime and Penal Policy; Reflections on Fifty Years Experience*. Allen and Unwin.

Chapter 4

Social work, psychiatry and criminal justice

Social work, psychiatry and their links with criminal justice were subjects on which Barbara Wootton gave considerable thought. In one of her lectures, she drew attention to what she called 'an extension to the sphere of medical authority'. She said it was no longer sufficient to render to God the things that are God's and to Caesar the things that are Caesar's. Both God and Caesar must now share their empires with the doctor.[1] It was not that she disapproved of such changes, more that she believed they produced complications and aberrations within the criminal justice system. For the problem was simply this: traditionally, violations of social norms were treated as matters that lay between a man's conscience and the criminal law. Now, such violations were more commonly held to involve questions of mental health or mental disorder.

Social work and social casework

In the late 1950s and early 1960s, psychiatric thinking was heavily influenced by the work of Sigmund Freud and his writings on psychoanalysis. So too was social work, probation and the other helping professions. This latter group may not have been able to claim the status or expertise of the psychiatrists, yet the terminology and mode of behaving showed their indebtedness to medical and psychoanalytic thought. Terms such as 'diagnosis treatment' and 'transference' were all part of the social workers' stock in trade, as were 'oedipal' and 'weaning' – the latter occurring when the members of the helping profession withdrew their interest in the client's affairs. The aim, as in all psychoanalytical thinking, was to provide the necessary insights into the clients' behaviour, and to release or remove those inner tensions which caused the clients to behave that way. In social work, this method or model was social casework, often defined in such terms, according to Barbara Wootton, as indicating 'lamentable arrogance'.

Barbara Wootton set about things with gusto. It is doubtful if there has been a more destructive criticism of social work, or the social work task as found in Chapter 9 of *Social Science and Social Pathology*. She began by comparing the numbers of social workers to barmen and barmaids, where according to the 1951 Census there were some 22,000 social workers, or slightly more than one social worker to every two barmen and barmaids.[2] The slight was obvious and clearly intended. However, much worse was to follow. She examined certain definitions of social casework, some of which she said were such that 'if taken at their face value, involve claims to powers which verge on omniscience', so that 'one can only suppose that those who perpetuate such claims must have been totally deserted by their sense of humour'.[3] She highlighted one definition as 'the art of assisting the individual in developing and making use of his personal capacity to deal with problems which he faces in his social environment' and another as 'the art of changing human attitudes'. In a third, 'the social worker shall seek to understand the person in need not only at that particular moment in time but also the pattern of personality the major experiences and relationships which make him the person he now is'. Faced with such claims, Barbara Wootton thought 'that the social worker's best and perhaps her only chance of achieving aims so intimate and so ambitious would be to marry the client'.[4]

To Barbara Wootton, these claims were pretentious – as were those that a two-year course in social work could lead to such heady heights. So in a debate on the Mental Health Bill (23 June 1959) in the House of Lords,[5] she informed their Lordships that the modern social worker was being trained 'to acquire a good understanding in the study of human needs, motivation, and behaviour'. She noted that the student in the two-year course is to get that good understanding of such matters. That being so, she wondered what she had missed.

> Some of us here have spent our whole lives in struggling how to make head or tail of human needs, motivation and behaviour, and it is a matter of regret to learn, so late, alas, in life for some of us, that had we but taken a two year course in social work training at the age of twenty, its mysteries would have been revealed to us.[6]

And elsewhere, she said, if social work training was so good and likely to produce such outstanding beneficial results, why restrict it? Why waste it on the working classes? Why not try it on a few world leaders?

She thought too that an obvious implication of social casework was it showed a complete disregard for basic practical problems, and in doing so accepted the status quo regarding the social situation of the client. For example, consider the plight of Mrs. A, who approached the social work agency seeking financial help for her baby. Her husband, it appeared, was in the habit of changing jobs regularly, and was often unemployed. For the social caseworker, trained to examine the deeper structures of human behaviour, it may appear that financial stringency was the ostensible motive for her visit. But according to social casework theory, this was far from the truth. For Mrs. A had in fact 'only a glimmering, being largely unconscious of her real needs'. Barbara Wootton was not impressed by this apparent deeper level of understanding. She thought it strange that 'anyone not imbued with the ideology of modern casework might have thought that women who are married to shiftless men are only too well aware of the fact'.[7]

Diagnosis was only part of the caseworker's task. In line with the commitment to psychoanalysis, and within that the medical model, treatment followed. Treatment was provided through the Relationship. That mystical entity was not to be confused with simple human friendship or friendliness, although as Barbara Wootton observed, artificial tricks of friendliness were used to create an impression of a hopeful and cheerful repose. The Relationship was the vehicle by which treatment was offered and determined. Without the Relationship, nothing could be expected or achieved; but with it, all was possible. The Relationship involved a complexity of feelings between social worker and client, which the client must 'work through'. This would almost always involve 'transference', i.e., the transfer of love to the social worker before arriving at a point of self-determination for the client. If handled successfully, the Relationship would move to its inevitable conclusion, but of course throughout the client and social worker had different parts to play. In typical, or rather classical, casework language, the client 'after floundering in indecision or premature decision would eventually create the inescapable moment when he must take over to himself responsibility for affirming through word or action, or both, that is the way it will be'.[8] In contrast, the social worker held 'the slower more rhythmic movement', a process reduced by Barbara Wootton to the prosaic when she said 'the social worker gets on with her knitting whilst the client makes up his mind'.[9]

Barbara Wootton was correct to draw attention to the claims and assertions that casework would produce such heady results, and do so by way of such an ideology, which incidentally had little empirical evidence to support it. It was the assumption that the social caseworkers understood their clients better than the clients understood themselves that was additionally objectionable. Social casework *was* pretentious nonsense, and it needed to be said. No one else had produced such a critique, and as far as I am aware, no one from the casework side of things has tried to defend it. The social work response, if there was one, has been to ignore it and continue as before. A lofty disdain has seemingly been the best form of defence.

Barbara Wootton, writing in 1978, said, 'Happily the phase of psycho analytic self deification gradually passed.'[10] Not according to Yvonne Johnson, who writing in 2008 about social work in America, said how there still remains a tendency to focus on psychological problems rather than try to intervene in the environment. Interestingly, she also said how rarely Barbara Wootton is cited in the USA, in spite of her use of American literature in her critique. Yet Johnson says Barbara Wootton's comments remain highly relevant in today's social work climate. 'Her questions about social work still beset the profession.'[11] And 'Clients especially those who expected practical assistance, have been exasperated by social workers stress on feelings.'[12]

It was not just the all-embracing nature of the social casework experience that brought forth Barbara Wootton's wrath, but the emphasis on psychiatric explanations to the exclusion of practical solutions. By concentrating on the deeper recesses of the client's psyche, there was the assumption that all was well elsewhere. It was the people that failed, not the system. Yet, social work, said Barbara Wootton, has always been for the poor, and will continue to be so, with the social worker's clients drawn overwhelmingly from the working classes. That means social work must always be about securing assistance for the disadvantaged, for 'if poverty was abolished the major part of social workers' functions would disappear.'[13] Accordingly, 'the primary task of a social worker is to see that our social services function efficiently, and that the benefits and services which they ostensibly provided reach those who are entitled to them'.[14] It was this that Barbara Wootton railed against: the refusal to accept that being disadvantaged was relevant, and by using psychoanalytical judgements, social workers explicitly blamed the client for the failings.

It is difficult to assess the full impact of Barbara Wootton's critique on social work training and practice. Clearly, and in spite of it, social casework has survived, yet probably not in the extreme forms as described in *Social Science and Social Pathology*. The temptation to deal with psychological problems rather than attack the more difficult social problems created by inequalities seems to have remained, presumably supporting the belief that psychological change may one day produce social change, and that if the client feels better, that is an improvement. Barbara Wootton did not see things that way; irrespective of the pretentious nature of social casework, it led, she thought, to a paternalistic view that 'Daddy knows best', and this was not the direction in which she thought social work should be going.[15]

Barbara Wootton's critique of social work practice has to be seen within a wider context of a culture dominant at the time. Social work and psychiatry shared similar interests; both were engaged in a similar therapeutic enterprise. They believed in the same Freudian view of the world, and hoped for the same therapeutic outcomes. They saw social problems as based on intrapsychic failings, and both implicitly and sometimes explicitly suggested that the external fabric was free of blame. This was what Barbara Wootton found unacceptable. Time and again she said the social workers' task was about providing social services to those who need them, and not, in the words of Virginia Woolf, to 'dabble their fingers, self approvingly in the stuff of other people's souls'.

Her critique of social work was written a decade or so before the changes made under the 1969 Children and Young Persons Act. This legislation removed the probation service from juvenile justice, placing the newly formed Social Services Departments at the centre of things. Needless to say, this was a dramatic change and a loss for the probation service, as at that time about one-third of all probation orders were on juveniles. In contrast, it provided a massive increase in the workload and prestige for social workers. Again, surprisingly, Barbara Wootton made little comment on this; yet these changes affected the image and work of social workers, and the image and work of the juvenile court, both of which were of great interest to her. Given her earlier criticism of social work training and practice, one might have thought the critique would have continued, especially as the legislation gave social workers the task of dealing with delinquent children. Another blind spot, perhaps.

It is not clear whether she approved or disapproved of such changes. In her book *Crime and Penal Policy*, published in 1978, she spent some time discussing the 1969 Children and Young Persons Act, including the role of social workers, the newly established Care Order to be undertaken by Local Authority social workers (which replaced the old Approved Schools) and the changes in court procedures. But she said nothing about the dominance of social services departments, or the introduction of the supervision order, which largely replaced the probation order for juveniles.

Nonetheless, and in spite of her approval of probation, she had a fairly low opinion of the value of probation reports. 'Cozy' and 'comforting' were the effects they produced, she said. The only related comment on the probation service was that she noted a reduction in the use of the probation orders. She was aware of the decline in the use of the probation order. So for example, in the Crown Court from 1966 to 1975, they were down from 17% to 7% for males, and from 43% to 24% for females – and in the Magistrates Courts, from 16% to 5% for males and from 24% to 11% for females. She suggested that some of the reasons for the reductions may be the courts saw probation as too soft, or the courts were becoming more interested in other noncustodial sentences, such as community service, but she did not see these changes as cause for alarm. She could not be expected to foresee the catastrophe that was to befall it in 2014 – no one could – but she should have seen it was already past its best.

Barbara Wootton's critique of social work and social casework made her few friends; the style and manner of the exercise assured her of that, but then she never sought friendships in that way. Did social work change as a result? Probably, yes. But psychoanalysis was a short-lived fashion; it has not entirely vanished of course, and social work training still retains a spectre of psychoanalytic thinking, as Yvonne Johnson testifies. What Barbara Wootton did was, I suspect, ensure that the more extreme claims were modified. That itself was a significant advance.

Mental health, mental disorder and responsibility in relation to crime

Barbara Wootton had a long-term interest in the mentally abnormal offender and the corresponding mental health legislation – which for these purposes means the 1959 and 1983 Mental Health Acts and the 1957 Homicide Act. In the House of Lords debate on the 1959 Mental Health Act, she said the problem for criminology had become a moral problem; the moral area consistently contracts and the medical area expands.[16] It was a trend which she thought had a huge impact on the way we view and treat offenders, whether in the courts or in our perception of crime.

Her arguments are found throughout numerous publications and lectures, but were essentially thus: the more we medicalise behaviour, the less people take responsibility for it. So, the intrusion of psychiatric concepts into areas which had hitherto been regarded as bad behaviour changes 'sin' into 'sickness'. The problem is compounded by the way mental illness or mental disorder has been so enlarged as to cover behaviour which would otherwise be called sinful. This extends the reach of psychiatry into areas once regarded as involving questions of morality. The power of psychiatrists would matter less if psychiatry were a science, but in the absence of any clear-cut definition, we have permitted psychiatrists to offer their own individual interpretations of what constitutes health or sickness. Granting the medical profession such latitude has, in Barbara Wootton's view, created a dangerous precedent as it gives psychiatrists unrestricted powers.[17]

Responsibility and the increasing influence of psychiatry

Barbara Wootton wrote in a paper entitled 'Sickness or Sin' that gone are the days

> when mental illness meant real madness: when the expert in mental medicine was invoked only to deal with violent or deluded persons, or those who were unmanageably hysterical, depressed to the point of total incapacity, or senile to the point of infantilism.[18]

Nowadays, she said, the contemporary psychiatrist is no longer exclusively occupied with such catastrophes but with a set of behavioural problems which would have once been regarded as sinful. This of itself, she said, would not matter; indeed, psychiatric interventions are often recognised as an advance whereby the psychiatrist has replaced the harsh and unyielding moralist. But Barbara Wootton said for as long as illness ranks as the perfect alibi for responsibility, enlarging and extending definitions of mental illness, and by implication extending the domain of medicine into these erstwhile areas, we explicitly change the nature of these activities and our explanations of them. The psychiatric patient, receiving treatment for that which was once a behavioural problem and hitherto the purview of the moralist, is, according to Barbara Wootton, thereby absolved of responsibility for actions relating to that behaviour – in which case these 'patients' cannot be blamed for those actions. And crime also becomes a different matter, whether in its interpretation, explanation or treatment.

She said numerous consequences follow. For example, if persons are no longer seen as responsible for their actions, might it be that there are fewer limitations, morally, to impose on their treatment – including decisions by the courts? Might it be that anything goes, as long as treatment is successful? And if we classify those offenders with behavioural problems as mentally ill, what of those nonoffenders with similar problems?

Are they also ill, or are they simply tiresome and unhappy? And how do such changes affect the law? Are we required to reshape our thinking to fit this new group of offenders and reshape mental health legislation accordingly? These are not questions asked nowadays, perhaps because the psychiatric influence that now pervades any discussion of antisocial behaviour is no longer felt to be obtrusive. This, said Barbara Wootton, is but a sign of its prevalence. It should not, however, be an indication of its unimportance. Understanding the forces that shape criminal justice is as relevant now as it ever was.

The problem begins with definitions, or rather the lack of suitable ones capable of adequately defining mental health and mental illness. Barbara Wootton asked, how could mental health and mental illness be defined in objective scientific terms, free of subjective moral judgements? For if not, then how can we have reliable criteria by which to distinguish the mentally healthy from this new group of mental patients called the mentally disordered? If there are no value-free definitions, was not the road then open for those who wish to classify all forms of antisocial behaviour, including criminal behaviour, as symptoms of mental disorder?[19] And would those so classified be free of responsibility whenever they exhibited those symptoms? Barbara Wootton thought we were already on that road, i.e., moving inexorably towards a position which advanced psychiatry and psychiatric ideology within the criminal justice system (including the other so-called helping professions) and in doing so include all forms of behaviour, deviant or otherwise, within its orbit. Failure to supply an objective definition would, she said, lead, *inter alia*, to the detriment of clarity and legal precision.

Barbara Wootton was not alone in asking such questions. Others, especially Thomas Szasz in America, had done so, and as a result been met with a frosty response from both medical and lay opinion. Barbara Wootton quoted him approvingly, seeing him as like-minded in his attempt to identify and control the power of psychiatrists. Both saw psychiatric intervention in penal policy in similar terms, namely that it was value-based, and according to Szasz when offered in the courts, was up for sale, i.e., that it could be purchased by either the defence or prosecution and paid for accordingly. Incidentally, I cannot find any reciprocal quotation by Szasz of Barbara Wootton. They were of course involved in a different narrative; Szasz was keen to argue that mental illness was a myth, that it was not a medical condition as it had no identifiable physiological base; it was simply a problem of living. To claim otherwise, said Szasz, was part of that psychiatric confidence trick by which psychiatrists plied their trade, maintained their status as members of the medical profession and duped those who were mad into believing they offered medical treatments. Barbara Wootton took a different approach; she was willing to use Szasz's arguments when it suited her, but she maintained more of a detached intellectual stance, producing less of a direct frontal attack on a particular professional group's ideology. Nonetheless, her criticisms of psychiatric practices were equally forceful and often more penetrating than those of the flamboyant Thomas Szasz.

When she examined numerous definitions of mental health, she found them wide-ranging. Almost all included a striking emphasis on the importance of individual members of society being satisfied with their lot, but most of all being part of and accepted within their current cultural milieu. It seems being mentally healthy meant having a 'healthy personality', which allowed the individual to function more or less perfectly in his/her current cultural milieu. Barbara Wootton found that many definitions of mental health were about fitting in to existing social networks, leading to 'a harmonious blending of the various emotions and character traits resulting in self control, and habits of conformity'. Fitting in meant not standing out, it being better to keep one's head down, for it seems 'mental health involves adapting to changing conditions without setting up conflicts or causing individuals to suffer pain or feel discomfort' – in other words, accepting the social world around us and not challenging the status quo. Barbara Wootton pointed out that none of these definitions were value-free; all were related to a local cultural pattern. So, being mentally healthy in Britain meant fitting into 'the standards of an acquisitive, competitive, hierarchical, envious society'. She noted also how often definitions of mental health express the personal value judgements of the authors. So, for example, a definition of mental health by the American Family Discussion Bureau was to define mental health in terms of a presumed ideal marital relationship, i.e., 'no undue dependence, passivity, aggression, or dominance on the part of either party, whereas definitions from the world of industry point to avoiding conflict (presumably industrial conflict) and thereby avoiding "bad mental hygiene"'.

As Barbara Wootton said, a 'harmonious blending to the cultural milieu' could allow a wholehearted Nazi to qualify as a mentally healthy person in a Nazi controlled society.[20] She added, 'fine phrases cannot obscure the fact that adjustment means adjustment to a particular culture, or to a particular set of institutions'.[21] There is a good example of this in that of a German criminologist who specified that psychopathic persons are those who refuse military service and are incurably litigious.[22]

Barbara Wootton's point is that to conceive adjustment in such terms is to identify health with the ability to come to terms with the culture, be it that of a totalitarian government, the dingy culture of an urban slum or the contemporary values of marriage – a point also made by Thomas Szasz, who said the psychiatrist, when practising in the Marriage Guidance Clinic, is explicitly emphasising the value of the institution of marriage. Criminality is therefore always a signal of maladjustment, whereby the law becomes an expression of the values of the society to which the individual must adjust to. Accordingly, there can be no opportunity or justification to rebel or argue that the law is wrong. (The suffragettes were clearly maladjusted and possibly mentally disordered in these terms.) According to these definitions, the mentally healthy person must always be in agreement with the existing dominant culture.

If mental health was difficult to define, or rather not be free of value judgements, what of its opposite, mental illness, or of the more general term mental disorder? Alas, according to Barbara Wootton, similar problems apply. She hoped otherwise as 'in principle on the grounds perhaps that in this vale of tears failure may be easier to identify than success'.[23] She found the most frequent definitions were by way of simply turning upside down those of mental health. Bowlby, for example, defines mental ill health to be 'derangement of the capacity to make cooperative relationships with other human beings'.[24] So, the mentally sick person would appear to be unhappy, at war with himself, inconsiderate, lacking in purpose, etc. Accordingly, one can see how in one definition a woman was diagnosed as 'neurotic', having recently 'embarked on her fourth marriage'. Barbara Wootton thought it far from clear how or why such matters could be medically established.

What then of the so-called maladjusted person, a term often used in the 1960s but less so nowadays? It was used then to describe someone who failed to accept current social norms, probably an offender but perhaps not a serious one. Here Barbara Wootton found similar problems. Definitions of the maladjusted person were such that he or she 'must learn to face reality', i.e., accept the norms and values of a competitive society. He/she must 'not achieve victories in phantasies', 'flee the memory of his/her failures', 'over indulge his/her children', but 'engage only in wholesome enjoyment', and 'learn to behave in a way that is prudent, rational, and with foresight'. In other words, do as you are told, cherish the values of individualism and accept that as a person you are responsible for your own destiny. According to these definitions, human welfare is attainable only by acceptance of local cultural norms and values. And of course adjustment is never complete; continual readjustment is necessary.

If, as it seems, no definition of mental health or mental illness is free of subjective, value-laden qualities, does it matter? The answer, according to Barbara Wootton, is that certain consequences follow – and they have an effect on criminology. One such consequence is that the label 'mentally ill' or 'mental disorder' can be applied merely because the person has failed to manage his/her life according to the accepted norms and values of society. So, if illness includes having four husbands, might it be that other forms of this woman's behaviour could also be classified as 'ill'? For without a clear definition of sickness or health, the road is wide open to call any disruptive behaviour an illness, giving unparalleled powers to psychiatrists and widening the concept of mental disorder to include any behaviour regarded as unseemly.

A second consequence is a restatement of the point made earlier, that conventional concepts of responsibility are undermined. 'Illness' implies a condition over which the individual has little or no control in the sense that it is not a matter of personal responsibility to be ill, except perhaps in those few cases where reckless behaviour may have helped induce that condition. So, said Barbara Wootton, if illness is inferred from bad behaviour, and as a result the person is no longer seen as responsible for actions related to that behaviour, it then follows that he/she can be absolved from responsibility from that and any other behaviour deemed to be an illness.

Of course, we have not moved far along that road as yet, but Barbara Wootton suggested we might be moving in that direction. Consider for example the Homicide Act 1957. This allows that a person who kills or is party to a killing shall not be convicted of murder if he was suffering from such abnormality of mind as substantially impaired his mental responsibility for his acts and omissions in doing or being party to the killing. In other words, not as in the McNaughton Rules because the offender did not appreciate the nature of the act, but because he has lost control over his actions.[25]

Nowhere is this better illustrated than in the inclusion of the psychopath as a form of mental disorder. Barbara Wootton saw the creation of this category of mentally disordered patients as the further encroachment of medicine into the province which was formerly reserved for morals.[26] The psychopath or sociopath – it is never clear if there was a difference – was included in the 1983 Mental Health Act. It was one of the four types of mental disorder – mental illness, arrested or incomplete development of mind being the others. Psychopathic disorder was defined under Section 5(2) as 'a persistent disorder or disability of mind (whether or not including significant impairment of intelligence) which results in abnormally aggressive or seriously irresponsible conduct on the part of the person concerned'.

Barbara Wootton said that defined in this way, 'psychopathy' makes nonsense of every attempt to distinguish the sick from the healthy, especially the sick and healthy criminal. It is, she said, also the model of the circular process by which mental abnormality is inferred from antisocial behaviour, while antisocial behaviour is explained by mental abnormality.[27] But the implications go beyond this: those classified as 'psychopathic' may once have been classified as 'extremely wicked'; today, they are considered to be mentally disordered – 'wicked' is no longer part of our lexicon of behaviours. Barbara Wootton saw the paradoxical effect of introducing a category of mental disorder such as 'psychopath' into our criminological language. If you are only moderately wicked, or show signs of repentance for your wickedness (i.e., have a conscience), you must expect to be punished for it, but if you are extremely wicked (psychopathic with no conscience), you may be seen as mentally disordered and excused responsibility, in which case you will receive treatment. 'So illogical a position can hardly, one would think, prove tenable for long.'[28] But it has; the 2007 Act retained the concept of 'psychopath' in spite of arguments otherwise.

It is not just the legal changes which reflect this developing mood which were upsetting, but, as said earlier, the way modern definitions of mental disorder include a great deal more than mere madness. Contemporary psychiatrists are now occupied by all manner of cases; the child psychiatrist deals with children who steal, have violent tempers or wet the bed, and the adult psychiatrist deals with neurotics, including 'the woman who had four husbands'. Psychiatrist patients include those who are complaining and complained about. They include children who behave badly, men and women who cannot manage their love affairs, criminals convicted of various offences as well as their victims, and those with irrational and sometimes rational fears.[29] Barbara Wootton makes the point that many of the symptoms for which psychiatric treatment is now sought are essentially behavioural problems, or in other words those diagnosed as mentally sick have in one way or another failed to manage their lives in the environment in which they live. Illness is inferred from the behaviour; indeed, illness *is* the behaviour. But, says Barbara Wootton, any disease, the morbidity of which is established only by the social failure that it involves, must rank as fundamentally different from those of which the symptoms are independent of social norms.[30]

Incidentally, it was not all gloom and doom. There were, she said, compensations. At a National Association of Mental Health Conference in London in 1962, she pointed out that one result of the growth of psychiatry has been to give wives of unfaithful husbands a new excuse: to say the poor man was sick was so much more acceptable than admitting he preferred another woman.[31],[32]

Nonetheless, the point remains: illness is now the behaviour. Does all this matter, and is it relevant nowadays? The answer depends on how much importance is given to notions of responsibility and morality. Barbara Wootton clearly thought they were important. She said,

> Not so long ago poverty crime and other social evils were explained as the product of shiftlessness, extravagance and indolence of the lower orders: it was the moral delinquencies of individuals (especially among the working classes) which were held responsible for problems of social disorientation. Today culpability is out of the fashion; the vogue is for traumatic experience. Today we have little idea who is sick and who is sinful.[33]

In this she is correct. We don't talk nowadays of 'sin'. Or of 'wickedness'. We call it bad behaviour, or perhaps call it 'criminal', and what was once called 'extreme wickedness' we now call 'psychopathy'. We talk of 'mental health', but we are no longer clear about the links, if any, with plain unhappiness; for example, if someone breaks up with his/her girlfriend/boyfriend and goes to his/her GP, the doctor will prescribe antidepressants, the implication being that there is a mental condition for what was once described as unhappiness. Aside from the long-term consequences that arise from prescribing highly addictive drugs for what are essentially 'problems of living', Barbara Wootton was right to call attention to that practice where the moral and medical merge.

What of the implications of the many psychiatric interventions in criminal justice? How do they affect the criminal justice system and by implication criminology? In the second of the papers cited earlier, i.e., in an address to Winchester College on 13 January 1963, Barbara Wootton expanded the argument. She said the medical profession is now required to fill three distinct roles in relation to the diagnosis and treatment of social deviants. The first is to consider within the framework of the criminal law the evidence on the mental state of accused persons and in particular on the degree in which they are to be held responsible and therefore punishable for their actions.[34] The second is to decide of those guilty of criminal offences whether they are suitable for medical rather than penal treatment. The third is to diagnose and treat types of mental disorders associated with unacceptable behaviour.

Of the three, the first is the one she considered most unsatisfactory. Barbara Wootton said it is unsatisfactory because again, it taints the medical with the penal, and thereby introduces ethical considerations in what purports to be purely expert medical evidence. She thought the crux of the matter was the inherent impossibility of making valid decisions about other people's responsibility. How does a psychiatrist, or anyone else for that matter, except perhaps the Almighty, determine how anyone could have acted otherwise? And as far as the law is concerned, how could anyone distinguish between the wicked and the weak-minded? But this is what psychiatrists are asked to do, and this is what they have agreed to do, which in Thomas Szasz's terms means deciding whether the offender is healthy enough to be punished.

No doubt psychiatrists over time develop 'a rule of thumb' type approach which provides some criterion satisfactory to themselves by which the wicked can be identified. But, said Barbara Wootton, even if the right criterion can be discovered, and there is general agreement about its rightness, it cannot be scientifically validated. There is no criterion to decide, in the face of conflicting evidence, whether the psychiatrist was right or wrong, except perhaps whether the offender subsequently committed further offences, but using recidivism as a guide is particularly unsatisfactory given the vagaries of relying on subsequent prosecutions. She thought the problem in law was particularly acute in cases of homicide, where questions of the responsibility of the offender at the time the offence was committed are exposed, that is to say before a verdict is reached. Other cases which raise questions about the mental health of the accused can be dealt with after conviction. These are themselves complicated but may lead to that other legal anomaly, a Hospital Order under the Mental Health Act 1983.[35] These apart, the overall problem was about deciding on questions of responsibility, and she said the doctor 'is not well cast as an authority on that'.[36]

The second problem is to decide which of those guilty of criminal offences are suitable for medical rather than penal treatment. This, said Barbara Wootton, constantly produces the unedifying spectacle of conflicts of professedly expert evidence, and lays upon the profession the duty of answering questions which are in the nature of things unanswerable. For the problems are this: what is the disease to be treated, and what is the hallmark of cure? Barbara Wootton put the question in the form of an offender who is convicted of theft but was depressed. Suppose the doctor succeeds in stopping the thieving but the depression continues: what then? Or perhaps the depression is cured but the thieving continues, in which case we have a cheerful rather than a depressed thief. But which of the results ranks as a cure? And anyway, the case illustrates what Barbara Wootton considers to be 'a profound change in the doctor's role when he assumes responsibility for the rehabilitation of offenders'. He no longer acts as a representative of the patient, but becomes an agent of the state and part of the machinery of law enforcement.

The third problem is that psychiatrists have powers to diagnose and treat types of mental disorder associated with unacceptable behaviour. Given the definition of psychopathy and that of mental illness in the legislation, let alone the lack of a satisfactory definition of mental illness, there is great scope for interpretation. Barbara Wootton says in the wide powers given to psychiatrists under the statutory definitions of the Mental Health Act, they come very near to having powers to make the law.

Taken together, these three features of psychiatric intervention illustrate the way its influence has permeated the workings of the courts and the confusion created by mixing the medical with the moral. Perhaps we care less about such matters nowadays where the heat has gone from the debate, but whether so or not, the questions remain. Take again the example of the depressed patient who commits an offence of shoplifting. Often we hear the depression is said to explain the theft. But how? What is there in being depressed that leads to, or causes, or accounts for the theft? Once upon a time, it was sin. Now we offer something different as an explanation, but no less satisfactory. And saying the person was depressed makes the offence more excusable, and thereby reduces individual responsibility, the centrepiece of the debate.

Psychiatry in criminal justice: the mental state of the accused

The second feature of 'responsibility' as used by Barbara Wootton was what she called 'the opposite aspect'. It was the way responsibility was used in the legal definition of crime, specifically as it applies to *actus reus* and *mens rea*.

As Herbert Hart (a famous Oxford lawyer) remarked in 1965, Barbara Wootton's name became synonymous with the claim that the whole doctrine of *mens rea* and the conception of responsibility embodied in it contained an irrational hindrance to sound social policy. He took a different view. Whilst he agreed with much of what Barbara Wootton said, he thought that *mens rea* underscored the values which are contained in a system of punishment, and as such should be preserved. This civilised disagreement between them produced what became known in the philosophy of law as the 'Wootton Hart' debate.[37] That debate was conducted in a most civilised manner but was nonetheless fierce and determined.

It began in one of Barbara Wootton's Hamlyn Lectures, *The Function of the Courts: Penal or Preventive*, and continued in a chapter in *Crime and Penal Policy* entitled 'Criminal responsibility and the mentally abnormal offender'. Barbara Wootton's position was thus: there is a choice between the punitive and preventive concept of the criminal process. In the punitive, the aim of the criminal law and the judicial process that follows is to punish the wicked – i.e., primarily retributive – whereas the aim within the preventive concept is to control action – a *Utilitarian* view. Supporters of the former, notably Lord Devlin, took the view that the aim of the criminal law was essentially punitive. The law itself comprised 'sins with legal definitions'. *Mens rea* was therefore fundamental to the punitive position; it being that a person who has caused a result which the criminal law forbids should be held responsible only if he intended to cause that result, or took a deliberate risk of causing it.[38] Only then can he be punished.

The debate hinged around that concept of 'responsibility'. It was used in a limited sense where, as defined by Barbara Wootton, it meant that a person was being able to act otherwise than he did,[39] or it was used in a more expansive way, where it meant being capable of controlling one's actions. The distinction is important and is best illustrated by the question 'Who broke the window?' Barbara Wootton simply wants to know who did it. Those supporting *mens rea* want to know not just 'who did it?' but 'did he intend to do it?' 'Intention' is the key word here; the defendant is responsible for the result because he deliberately chose to cause it, or because he deliberately chose to take an unreasonable risk of causing it.

It has long since been a fundamental principle of English law that there should be two components to a criminal offence: *actus reus* and *mens rea*, the former being the act itself and the latter being a guilty intention. This means that a person who has caused a result which the criminal law forbids (say, breaking the window) should be held responsible only if he intended to cause that result or took a deliberate risk of causing it.[40] The defendant is responsible for the result because he deliberately chose to take an unreasonable risk of causing it. An implication of this is that it is possible to determine whether committing that crime (breaking that window) was conscious and wilful, and to assess the measure of guilt if it was. A small number of criminal offences in English law do not require *mens rea* to be present. These are absolute offences, or offences of strict liability. An example of a strict liability offence would be driving without insurance. It matters not that the driver thought he was insured or never intended to drive without insurance; it is sufficient for the prosecution that he did not have insurance. Generally speaking, offences of strict liability are reserved for relatively minor offences.

Barbara Wootton wished to establish that there should be no general presumption that *mens rea* was to be a necessary element in criminality, or in other words, she wished to abolish *mens rea* and turn all criminal offences into offences of strict liability. She did not wish to do so immediately; rather, she wanted to allow it to wither away, thereby permitting strict liability offences to dominate. In her view, the mental state of the offender at the time of committing the offence would be considered after the conviction, and used only for the purpose of determining the appropriate sentence and/or treatment. So, to determine the conviction was to determine who broke the window.

The proposals met with a vigorous response from numerous senior lawyers, producing what one lawyer called 'great soul searching', and leading him to 'think furiously about matters which he and other lawyers had previously taken for granted'.[41] Barbara Wootton thought part of the muddle we get ourselves into is to produce a hybrid system of criminal justice. Some of it involves *mens rea*, some of it involves strict liability, and some offer an insanity defence.[42] After all, she said, it matters not to the victim whether the offender intended to commit the crime. The victim sees the harm done, and finds satisfaction in a sentence which prevents further such actions.

She also asked if it mattered whether someone who has committed a prohibited act did or did not do so intentionally. She thought that traditionalists ask the law to reinstate a moralist view of punishment, whereby if the action was not intentional it would be morally wrong to punish the offender. Her proposal would therefore remove that punitive tradition, as it was not the law's business to punish the wicked but to prevent future criminality – hence her view that *mens rea* should come after the decision was made that an offence had been committed, and not before.

Why adopt such a system? Barbara Wootton argued that whether a man who has broken the law could have acted differently is in principle unworkable. She argued that science cannot assess the appropriate 'denunciatory' value of a sentence – this a shot at Lord Devlin. She asks, how can anyone assess the offender's state of mind at the time of the offence? How can anyone say with any degree of certainty that an offender intended to do this, and not to do that? There is no scientific test which has been devised which can discriminate between offenders who are responsible and those who are not. Her view still involved some assessment of the offender's intention, albeit after conviction, but it would only be by way of establishing a propensity to commit crime. She thought it a fallacy to infer more than that. Decisions about intention or responsibility, she said, can only be by making a number of assumptions based on one's own knowledge or experience and 'putting oneself in the offender's shoes'. And anyway, the aim of the criminal law is prevention of socially damaging actions. *Mens rea* makes sense only within a retributive theory of punishment, and as Barbara Wootton was a Utilitarian, it was no surprise that she saw things differently.

She was faced with two formidable legal opponents, Professor Herbert Hart and Professor John Smith – the latter was a famous criminal lawyer and contributor to her *Festchrift*. The former she described as liberal and therefore was surprised that he 'seems incurably obsessed with the notion of punishment which haunts his text'; and 'although rejecting many traditional theories such as that punishment should be retributive or denunciatory he [Professor Herbert Hart] nevertheless seems wholly unable to envisage a system in which sentence is not automatically equated with punishment'.[43]

Professor Hart puts it this way:

> once it has been established that a person's conduct is comprised in the definition of some crime, this without any proof of *mens rea* would be sufficient for conviction, and to try him within the ambit of compulsory measures to be chosen by the court. The choice between the measures would not be made by reference to the offender's state of mind at the time of the crime; the sole question for consideration would be the minimum action in view of his present psychological state, character and situation is likely to prevent the recurrence of the offence.[44]

Professor Hart says that Barbara Wootton offers a system of punishment which turns out to be a purely forward-looking form of social hygiene. It deals with the offender's future and the prevention of his future criminality, but ignores the deterrent effect on others. He sees the distinction we make under *mens rea*, before convicting a sane offender as providing an elementary safeguard. Under Barbara Wootton's proposals, unintentional and accidental wrongdoing would no longer be a defence before conviction. So to show that an accused had accidentally wounded another would not be a defence and would not save him from conviction, or from the liability to be given preventive treatment.[45] He says,

> In such a system once it has been established that a person's outward conduct is comprised in the definition of some crime, this without

> proof of *mens rea* would be sufficient for conviction and to try him within the ambit of compulsory measures to be chosen by the courts. The choice between these measures (Penal or medical) would not be made by reference to the offender's state of mind at the time of his crime, the sole question for consideration would be the minimum action in view of his present psychological state, character and situation, is likely to prevent the recurrence of the offence.[46]

Professor Hart's view was that Barbara Wootton offered a system where the aim was primarily to deal with the offender's future and the prevention of further crime. Professor Hart asked, why did Barbara Wootton wish to adopt such a system? He thought the answer was clear; her objections were all part and parcel of the same package; that is to say, a scientific approach should be brought to the law and sentencing in the same way as it is necessary to introduce a scientific approach to other aspects of the social world. She said it was not possible for anyone to decide whether at the time of the offence the offender was responsible for his actions. She quoted approvingly the comment by the Lord Chief Justice, Lord Parker, who said the step between, 'he did not resist his impulse' and 'he could not resist his impulse' is one which is incapable of scientific proof.[47] Apparently, in an attempt to solve the unsolvable, the learned judge went on to invoke common sense to make good the deficiencies of science. The question for medical men (and others) remains: by what criteria are we to decide whether an offender was, at the time of the offence, wicked or mad? Or both? Or neither?'[48]

Professor Smith shared Professor Hart's reservations. He believed Barbara Wootton's proposal would remove the criminal law as a moral force and create a dangerous vacuum. He said it would empty the law of its moral content. Professor Smith said *mens rea* offers consideration of personal freedom. If *mens rea* were abolished, every blow (assault) would have to be investigated. It would lead to an expansion of police powers and greater uncertainty for the individual. Moreover, the law would lose its authority and the odium of an offence. It would mean losing certain crimes from the statute book which were available under *mens rea*, such as crimes which were attempts, i.e., attempted murder, attempted assault, conspiracy to commit fraud, etc. In Professor Hart's view, what 'distinguishes an attempt which fails from an innocent activity is that it is a step taken with the intention of bringing about some harmful consequence'.[49]

There was no doubt that Barbara Wootton's proposals would meet opposition from most lawyers, brought up in an atmosphere described by John Smith as producing firm adherents to the doctrine of *mens rea*. He, like many others, would not wish to say that doctrine was without criticism, but the alternative as proposed by Barbara Wootton, he would say, would produce rather more blemishes – not the least that it would mean the police would be required to investigate and probably prosecute acts which are regarded as due to carelessness, negligence or even accidents. Of course, Barbara Wootton had a point when she said it was not possible for anyone to decide whether at the time of the offence the offender was responsible for his actions. And citing the example of 'the irresistible impulse' gave strength to her argument, as did her point that there is no scientific test which have been devised which can discriminate offenders who are responsible and those who are not, but more than this is required to get a purposeful change in legal thinking and practice.

She was also correct to point out that there are certain defences in mental health legislation that operate without *mens rea*. But these are small in number and affect few offenders. To see these as part of a trend away from *mens rea* is disingenuous, they being for a selected group of offenders. What seems to have upset Professor John Smith, and what he called 'shocking', was the suggestion that the concept of criminal responsibility 'be allowed to wither away'.[50] It was too soon and altogether too radical a proposal.

Herbert Hart said there was also 'an almost total ignorance of the deterrent effect on potential offenders' in Barbara Wootton's proposals.[51] He was correct to point to this limitation, and she was equally correct when she gloomily recorded that we are in for a period in which the traditional moralistic and punitive attitude will dominate the penal process.[52]

In spite of this measure of disagreement, both lawyers were fulsome in their praise of her. Herbert Hart said her book was 'remarkable by a remarkable Englishwoman', and John Smith praised her for making him 'think furiously about what she had said'. The debate will no doubt continue, although in this particular battle it seems the lawyers have the edge.

An assessment

Barbara Wootton's contribution to the debate on mental disorder and crime is both thought-provoking and interesting. It was wide ranging, concerned with the impact on criminology and on the law, and including questions of human rights. Looking back over 50 years or so from the time she was writing, it is possible to argue that her concerns were overemphasised and slightly misplaced. 'The road down which we were travelling' leading to a greater measure of psychiatric influence and control has not widened, nor does it seem to have been extended. Fears about psychiatric intrusion and concerns about a loss of responsibility seem less important nowadays. To some extent, this has been due to the psychiatrists themselves; they have shown less interest in extending their domain than was once thought. And the term 'psychopathy' is increasingly seen as approximating more of a moral judgement, and a defect of learning and socialisation rather than an illness. Many psychiatrists use it in the vernacular and as a term of derogation. Not all do, of course, but it is regarded by most as indicating nothing more than that the patient is untreatable. In this respect, psychiatrists have outrun legislators. Psychiatric treatments may have been extended to cover a multitude of behaviours, but they have also been accompanied by a concern for the patient, often expressed as sympathy for his/her condition. This has been accompanied with a tempered assessment of the effectiveness of their treatments. To quote Barbara Wootton yet again: 'No matter who has the first word the last is always with the statistician',[53] and the statistician has not always been kind to the psychiatrist. Report after report shows that psychiatric intervention into criminality does no better than other interventions – or no worse – and is no more successful than other interventions in inducing favourable modifications of deplorable behaviour. This too may mean we see psychiatry as less of a threat than Barbara Wootton did.

Nor does it seem we are concerned nowadays about a loss of responsibility. Terms such as 'wicked' or 'moral' are not part of our vocabulary – perhaps due to that same psychiatric influence – with little interest to be protected from such trends. Yet Barbara Wootton was correct to draw attention to such changes; she saw, as few others did, that psychiatric explanations changed traditional ways of explaining behaviour, especially criminal behaviour, and that what we now take for granted was new and able to break the existing mould. She saw too the possible implication that removing responsibility opened the way for a more authoritarian technological system of control, which freed control agents from considerations of matters other than what was technically possible and what was ultimately effective. Without responsibility, Samuel Butler's 'Erewhon' must be the feared model for the future.

She seems not to have had much influence in her opposition to the general proposition that there should be more restraints on the activities of the medical profession generally, or more specifically in more restraints on practices in criminal justice. For example, in the House of Lords debates on the 1959 Mental Health Act, the Bill proposed that decisions to compulsorily detain patients should no longer be considered by the courts but left entirely to the medical and social work professions.

Barbara Wootton opposed this; she was concerned that this provided too few restraints on the medical practitioners. She concluded that 'perhaps there was a tendency to endow the medical man with some of the attributes that are supposed elsewhere to inhere in the medicine man'.[54] Her objections had little support amongst other members, yet she made an important point. With no right of appeal against the wishes of one medically qualified person and one social worker who may or may not be qualified according to the precepts of social work training, the unfortunate patient can be compulsorily admitted to a mental hospital, and if need be further detained by the decision of two medical officers and one social worker. Barbara Wootton wanted the patient to have the opportunity to appear before a court to register an appeal against being 'sectioned'. Her instincts were, in my view, correct; there was and is too little restraint on the activities of the medical profession under powers granted by the Mental Health Act.

She was also unsuccessful in her bid to reduce the impact of *mens rea* on the legal system, and a corresponding reduction on criminal responsibility. It is likely that she found few supporters within the legal profession generally, liberals included.[55] She may have caused certain eminent lawyers to 'think furiously', but they were reluctant to change their ways; *mens rea* is here to stay and that, for them, is the end of it.

Yet she was certainly correct to see the problem of criminology as a moral problem where the moral area consistently contracts and the medical area expands.[56] She was also correct to identify a trend and explain some of the implications whereby mental ill health is seen to be ever wider in its definition, and its opposite, morality, is becoming ever smaller. That this has been hardly noticed elsewhere in criminology is a testament to Barbara Wootton.

Notes

1 Wootton B (1992) The law, the doctor and the deviant. Reprinted In Seal V and Bean P (eds) *Barbara Wootton Selected Writings Vol. 2 Crime and the Penal System* p. 61.
2 Wootton B (1959) *Social Science and Social Pathology*. George Allen and Unwin p. 268.
3 Ibid. p. 271.
4 Ibid. pp. 271, 273.
5 House of Lords Debates on Mental Health Bill Hansard 23 June 1959 Vol. 217 cols. 91–48.
6 Ibid. col. 104.
7 Wootton B (1959) *Social Science and Social Pathology*. George Allen and Unwin. op. cit. p. 278.

8 Ibid. p. 281.
9 Ibid.
10 Wootton B (1992) The social work task today. Reprinted In Seal V and Bean P (eds) *Barbara Wootton Selected Writings Vol. 2 Crime and the Penal System* p. 169.
11 Johnson YM (2008) Remembering Barbara Wootton's contribution to social work education. *Journal of Social Work Education* Vol. 44 No. 1 p. 24.
12 Ibid. p. 30.
13 Wootton B (1992) The social work task today. Reprinted In Seal V and Bean P (eds) *Barbara Wootton Selected Writings Vol. 2 Crime and the Penal System.* op. cit. p. 171.
14 Ibid. p. 172.
15 Wootton B. (1992) Daddy knows best. Reprinted In Seal V and Bean P (eds) *Barbara Wootton Selected Writings Vol. 2 Crime and the Penal System* pp. 156–167.
16 House of Lords Debates on mental Health Bill. Hansard 23 June 1959 Vol. 217 col. 716.
17 Wootton B (1978) *Crime and Penal Policy; Reflections on Fifty Years Experience.* Allen and Unwin p. 220.
18 Wootton B (1992) Sickness or sin? Reprinted In Seal V and Bean P (eds) *Barbara Wootton Selected Writings Vol. 2 Crime and the Penal System* p. 76.
19 Chapter 8. Wootton B (1959) *Social Science and Social Pathology*. George Allen and Unwin. op. cit.
20 Ibid. p. 215.
21 Ibid. p. 218.
22 House of Lords Debates on Mental Health Bill. Hansard 23 June 1959 Vol. 217 col. 719.
23 Wootton B (1959) *Social Science and Social Pathology*. George Allen and Unwin. op. cit. p. 221.
24 Ibid. p. 222.
25 Ibid. p. 233.
26 House of Lords Debates on Mental Health Bill. Hansard 23 June 1959 Vol. 217 cols. 91–148.
27 Wootton B (1959) *Social Science and Social Pathology*. George Allen and Unwin. op. cit. p. 250.
28 Ibid. p. 251.
29 Ibid. p. 222.
30 Ibid. p. 225.
31 Oakley A (2011) *A Critical Woman*. Bloomsbury Academic p. 262.
32 The 1983 Act excluded people from being dealt with 'by reason only of promiscuity or other immoral conduct, sexual deviancy or dependence on alcohol or drugs'. The amended Act, the Mental Health Act 2007, contains an exclusion only by virtue of 'dependence on alcohol or drugs'. It was considered that society's views of what constitutes promiscuity and immoral conduct – and how it should be regarded – have changed significantly over the past 25 years, and the government assumed that no professionals would ever use the Act to detain and treat someone purely on these grounds. However, the removal of 'sexual deviancy' does allow paedophiles to come within the scope of the Act so long as they fulfil all the conditions for its use. The Act also

excludes people with a learning disability, 'unless that disability is associated with abnormally aggressive or seriously irresponsible conduct'.

The main change from the 1983 Act concerns a patient's 'treatability' under Section 3. Under the original 1983 Act, detention and treatment on grounds of mental impairment or psychopathic disorder could be authorised only if it was considered that treatment was 'likely to alleviate or prevent a deterioration' of the patient's condition. The government was concerned that some people with a personality disorder who were perceived to be a danger to the public might not be detained because clinicians could argue that there was no treatment they could offer that would meet this requirement. Accordingly, this has been replaced by the requirement for availability of 'appropriate medical treatment'.

33 Wootton B (1992) Sickness or sin? Reprinted In Seal V and Bean P (eds) *Barbara Wootton Selected Writings Vol. 2 Crime and the Penal System*. op. cit. p. 83.

34 Wootton B (1992) The law, the doctor and the deviant. Reprinted In Seal V and Bean P (eds) *Barbara Wootton Selected Writings Vol. 2 Crime and the Penal System*. op. cit. p. 61.

35 A Hospital Order can be made under Section 37(1) of the Mental Health Act 2007. It says, 'Where a person is convicted before the Crown Court of an offence punishable with imprisonment other than an offence the sentence for which is fixed by law, . . . or is convicted by a magistrates' court of an offence punishable on summary conviction with imprisonment, and the conditions mentioned in subsection (2) below are satisfied, the court may by order authorise his admission to and detention in such hospital as may be specified in the order or, as the case may be, place him under the guardianship of a local social services authority or of such other person approved by a local social services authority as may be so specified.'

36 Wootton B (1992) The law, the doctor and the deviant. Reprinted In Seal V and Bean P (eds) *Barbara Wootton Selected Writings Vol. 2 Crime and the Penal System*. op. cit. p. 65.

37 Oakley A (2011) *A Critical Woman*. Bloomsbury Academic. op. cit. p. 261.

38 Smith J (1986) Responsibility in criminal law. In Bean PT and Whynes D (eds) *Barbara Wootton. Social Science and Public Policy. Essays in her Honour*. Tavistick p. 142.

39 Wootton B (1972) Crime responsibility and prevention. In Gerber R and McAnany P (eds) *Contemporary Punishment*. University of Notre Dame Press p. 170.

40 Smith J (1986) Responsibility in criminal law. In Bean PT and Whynes D (eds) *Barbara Wootton. Social Science and Public Policy. Essays in her honour*. Tavistick. op. cit. p. 141.

41 Ibid.

42 These occur where the accused is proved to have committed a crime but claims a defence under the McNaughton Rules and is found to be not guilty by reason of insanity. Or, under the Mental Health Act where in Section 60 a Magistrates' Court can make a Hospital or Guardianship Order against an accused without recording a conviction against him if the court is satisfied he did the act with which he is charged. See Wootton B (1978) *Crime and Penal Policy; Reflections on Fifty Years Experience*. Allen and Unwin. op. cit. p. 225.

43 Wootton B (1963) *Crime and the Criminal Law: Reflections of a Magistrate and a Social Scientist*. (The Hamlyn Lectures) Stevens and Sons. (Second Edition 1981 with postscripts to each chapter) p. 50.
44 Hart HL (1965) *Book Review Yale Law Journal* Vol. 74 p. 1327.
45 Ibid. p. 1328.
46 Ibid. p. 1327.
47 Wootton B (1992) The law, the doctor and the deviant. Reprinted In Seal V and Bean P (eds) *Barbara Wootton Selected Writings Vol. 2 Crime and the Penal System*. op. cit. p. 65.
48 Wootton B (1963) *Crime and the Criminal Law: Reflections of a Magistrate and a Social Scientist*. (The Hamlyn Lectures) Stevens and Sons. (Second Edition 1981 with postscripts to each chapter). op. cit. p. 73.
49 Hart HL (1965) *Book Review Yale Law Journal* Vol. 74 p. 1329. op. cit.
50 Smith J (1986) Responsibility in criminal law. In Bean PT and Whynes D (eds) *Barbara Wootton. Social Science and Public Policy. Essays in her Honour*. Tavistick. op. cit. p. 142.
51 Hart HL (1965) *Book Review Yale Law Journal* Vol. 74 p. 1328. op. cit.
52 Smith J (1986) Responsibility in criminal law. In Bean PT and Whynes D (eds) *Barbara Wootton. Social Science and Public Policy. Essays in her Honour*. Tavistick. op. cit. p 141.
53 Wootton B (1959) *Social Science and Social Pathology*. George Allen and Unwin. op. cit. p. 252.
54 Mental Health Bill 4 June 1959 Vol. 216 cols. 666–768 col. 717.
55 Wootton B (1978) *Crime and Penal Policy; Reflections on Fifty Years Experience*. Allen and Unwin. op. cit. p. 224.
56 Mental Health Bill 4 June 1959 Vol. 216 cols. 666–768 col. 721. op. cit.

References for publications by Barbara Wootton

A more complete list of Barbara Wootton's publications can be found in Seal V and Bean P.T. (1992) (eds) *Barbara Wootton. Selected Writings*. MacMillan Vols 1–4.

Wootton B (1950) *Testament for Social Science*. George Allen and Unwin.

Wootton B (1959) *Social Science and Social Pathology*. George Allen and Unwin.

Wootton B (1962) *A Social Scientists Approach to Maternal Deprivation in Deprivation of Maternal Care; A Reassessment of Its Effects*. WHO pp. 63–73.

Wootton B (1963) *Crime and the Criminal Law: Reflections of a Magistrate and a Social Scientist* (The Hamlyn Lectures) Stevens and Sons. (Second Edition 1981 with postscripts to each chapter).

Wootton B (1967) *In a World I Never Made. Autobiographical Reflections*. George Allen and Unwin.

Wootton B (1972) Crime responsibility and prevention. Reprinted In Gerber R and McAnany D (eds) *Contemporary Punishment*. University of Notre Dame Press pp. 164–175.

Wootton B (1978) *Crime and Penal Policy; Reflections on Fifty Years Experience.* Allen and Unwin.
Wootton B (1992) The administration of justice. Lecture given to the University of Leeds. Reprinted In Seal V and Bean P (eds) *Barbara Wootton Selected Writings Vol. 1 Crime and the Penal System* pp. 95–108.
Wootton B. (1992) Some reflections on the first five years of community service. Reprinted In Seal V and Bean P (eds) *Barbara Wootton Selected Writings Vol. 1 Crime and the Penal System* pp. 143–145.
Wootton B (1992) Who are the criminals? Reprinted In Seal V and Bean P (eds) *Barbara Wootton Selected Writings Vol. 1 Crime and the Penal System* pp. 109–117.
Wootton B (1992) Time and the drug scene. Reprinted In Seal V and Bean P (eds) *Barbara Wootton Selected Writings Vol. 1 Crime and the Penal System* pp. 135–137.
Wootton B (1992) Sickness or sin? Reprinted In Seal V and Bean P (eds) *Barbara Wootton Selected Writings Vol. 2 Crime and the Penal System* pp. 76–84.
Wootton B (1992) The law, the doctor and the deviant. Reprinted In Seal V and Bean P (eds) *Barbara Wootton Selected Writings Vol. 2 Crime and the Penal System* pp. 61–75.
Wootton B (1992) Psychiatry ethics and the law. Reprinted In Seal V and Bean P (eds) *Barbara Wootton Selected Writings Vol. 2 Crime and the Penal System* pp. 1–12.

Chapter 5

An assessment

Barbara Wootton's legacy as a criminologist

Barbara Wootton's contribution to criminology was in three major areas: first through her lectures and publications, second through her memberships (and often chairmanship of government committees) and finally through the House of Lords. Her media contributions were also important, if only because they meant she was instantly recognised as a public figure inducing a measure of affection. Someone described her 'almost a household name in contemporary Britain'.[1] Taken together, her contributions during her lifetime were such as to suggest she was someone of immense influence. When she published her Autobiography *In a World I Never Made*, a number of reviewers thought she was being disingenuous. A member of the House of Lords observed, 'She may feel that; but I don't believe I am alone in finding myself in a world that she greatly influenced.'

In whatever setting she found herself, Barbara Wootton was a severe critic of existing practices and procedures. This was particularly so in her written work, whether in criminology, economics or public policy. Yet in criminology (and elsewhere), it was not simply criticism for criticism's sake, but to advance the subject matter, albeit it in a specific direction. As said earlier, that direction was based on a Utilitarian view of society, with a methodology directly drawn from John Stuart Mill's *System of Logic* (published in 1843). Mill referred to what he called 'the moral sciences' as 'those areas of study having to do with human dispositions, character, and action, extending from psychology to social science'. He then applied this approach to social science, which he thought should be aimed at the discovery of general causal laws based on systematic empirical observation.

In *Testament for Social Science* and in numerous other publications, Barbara Wootton followed that path. The mantra was that knowledge should be accumulated and applied to all branches of the social sciences, including criminology. The scientific method was, she said, 'simply the attempt to acquire knowledge of general laws directly or indirectly by experience by the use of our five senses'.[2] She thought that social science, including criminology, could help achieve greater control over our environment so that the most magnificent conquest of all may be achieved.[3] Her criticisms were aimed at promoting that conquest.

It could be said she was fortunate to live at a time when criminology was at an early stage of development and therefore more readily open to criticism. She was one of the few in Britain who saw its potential, and her criticisms were based on the assumption that the subject could progress. Certainly, in the 1950s there were few empirical studies on which to base a critique, but there were enough, and it was a growing discipline. Without going into a detailed history of British criminology, it is worth noting that in Barbara Wootton's early years, i.e., the 1920s and beyond, there was hardly anything written which could be called 'criminology', or indeed little of social science generally. Barbara Wootton reminds us that at the time she graduated, in the early 1920s, virtually the only available approach to the academic study of social problems was economics. Almost the whole of the work that occupied the academies was of a deductive, not an inductive, character, with the result that the products of those academies were hopelessly ill equipped to undertake any kind of social investigation.[4] Thirty years later, in the 1950s in Britain, there had not been a great deal of change, although it was possible to see signs of some improvement.

Also, there had been no tradition of criminology in Britain at least until the mid-1950s, or perhaps slightly earlier when it was introduced by a small number of lawyers and psychiatrists from Continental Europe. Hermann Mannheim, a jurist, wrote on *Social Aspects of Crime in England Between the Wars*, a pathfinding project being one of the first empirical studies of crime in Britain. Max Gruenhut, a psychiatrist, was interested in developing the probation system which was hitherto based on the London Police Court Missionaries, and Leon Radzinowicz, a lawyer who became the Foundation Professor at the Institute of Criminology, Cambridge, argued for a more empirical approach. Finally, Emanuel Miller, another psychiatrist, often called the father of British child psychiatry, introduced one of the earliest child guidance clinics. Their influence was important as it formed the basis of later criminological thinking, but in the 1950s it remained within a ratified circle. Criminology then was not a subject with a great deal of appeal.[5]

In fact, apart from this group of innovators, the literature, such as there was, especially in sociology, came almost entirely from America. Subcultural theory was popular at the time, as was Edwin Sutherland's theory of differential association, as it still is today. Labelling theory, which changed the criminological landscape, did not arrive in Britain until 1968, a decade after *Social Science and Social Pathology* was published, and this too was American. The British approach such as there was in the 1950s, when Barbara Wootton reviewed the literature, was dominated by concerns about the 'causes of crime', which largely meant asking what factors led to delinquency. The answers were thought to lie largely within the family, so the 'broken home' in its various forms dominated thinking.

It was in this milieu that Barbara Wootton wrote *Testament for Social Science* (published in 1950) and *Social Science and Social Pathology* (published in 1959). She hoped as a result of her research there would be a day when criminological expertise would be publicly accepted and where current clichés such as 'delinquency is all the fault of the parents' or that 'punishment makes a man worse not better' (or perhaps the other way round!) are simply worthless unless supported by the evidence.[6] Her criticisms of the studies listed in *Social Science and Social Pathology* were trenchant; the studies themselves centred around 'the popular current hypotheses about the causes or the characteristics of crime and delinquency'.[7] The questions being asked in those studies were uncomplicated, and the methodologies likewise.

Nonetheless, what was available was important at the time, and whilst from a distance they now seem limited, and perhaps even a little naïve, they were not so in the 1950s. Her critique was important if only to show, in David Downes's terms, that it helped usher in a far more adventurous phase of criminological enquiry, adding that even if this phase is spent, the insights afforded should not be lost.[8] Her biographer takes a different view, more pessimistic about her impact on criminology; namely, that criminology never recovered from Barbara Wootton's allegations that opinion is not the same as systematically tested knowledge.[9]

One of Barbara Wootton's major contributions to criminology is found throughout this critique; it showed a fearsome determination to point where those selected studies failed, a refusal to accept anything that did not reach a certain standard, and a passion for the subject matter, all based on a clear methodology. All of these pointed to a future for criminology, albeit under a certain banner and in a certain direction, but a future nonetheless – that is, if later criminologists wished to go in that direction. What Barbara Wootton did was to break new ground and do so with a certain elegance and clarity.

It was that ability to ask difficult questions and seek out implications for practice that set her apart. She asked questions that others had not asked, and perceived implications that others did not perceive. She was one of the first to point out that the typical offender was the motoring offender,[10] that the juvenile court system was in need of reform and that the influence of psychiatry had changed the nature and view of human responsibility. Also that favoured terms like 'irresistible impulse' in mental health legislation was incapable of scientific verification; was an irresistible impulse one that was irresistible or one that was not resisted? We shall never know, said Barbara Wootton. As Professor John Smith said of Barbara Wootton's criticism of 'the cherished doctrine of *mens rea*', where again she said a 'guilty mind' was also incapable of scientific verification, she caused others to think furiously about matters they had previously taken for granted.[11] As a result, criminology, including penal policy, was fundamentally altered, whether it be regarding the role of punishment, the introduction of new services or perceptions of trends in the interpretation of events.

Implicit in almost all her writings was a pioneering spirit. She spoke often of working for the public good, sometimes almost with an old-fashioned, puritanical fervour. She would not, of course, ascribe to the direct religious component of that aphorism; she was an active humanist, being a member and founder of a number of humanist organisations, but her humanism had a deep-seated passion which nonetheless was almost evangelical.[12] In the Epilogue of her Autobiography, she wrote she had often the satisfaction of seeing the laughable idealism of one generation evolve into the accepted commonplace of the next. 'But it is from the champions of the impossible rather than the slaves of the possible that evolution draws its creative force.'[13]

In this respect, she was a pioneering criminologist. That is to say, she hoped for and had expectations for a better world, and campaigned accordingly, whether in her publications or public pronouncements. In her Autobiography, she wrote that human tragedy was due to our failure to master the social world as we have mastered the physical world.[14] It was a pioneering approach, unashamedly optimistic, placing criminology within that optimism.

Her campaigning force was assisted by another of her strengths, her style of writing. It is difficult to describe it, but it is instantly recognisable.

Often it had within it a biting wit but was always a delight to read, unless of course one was the recipient of her sarcasm. Her style was such that she rarely quoted from other people's work: she may occasionally have drawn attention to other views, but I cannot think of many examples where she used a direct quote to support her own position. Moreover, the mental images she created were extraordinary, whether of the social worker 'getting on with her knitting' or the pretentions of psychiatrists, where 'there is no form of social deviation in an individual which psychiatrists will not treat' – or of the motoring offender, where she suggested closer psychiatric attention should be given to the persistent parking offender. 'Might it be that he has been committing his offences due to having been snatched untimely from his mother's breast'?[15]

It was a style of writing that held the reader's attention, always with an expectation that there would be a sting somewhere, probably at the end. And often there was. Two passages from *Social Science and Social Pathology* in her critique of social work illustrate the point. The first, also quoted earlier, is about Mrs. A, who called the social work agency but

> [H]er real needs are found to be quite different; she is in fact dissatisfied with her position as the wife of a man who does not support her or care for her as a really masculine man might be expected to do. Of this area of her difficulties Mrs A. is 'only to have a glimmering,' being largely unconscious of her real needs, – although anyone not imbued with the ideology of modern casework might have thought that women who are married to shiftless men are generally only too well aware of the fact.[16]

The second concerns claims by social workers that the modern social caseworker was

> trained to understand the person in need, not only at that particular moment in time but also the pattern of the clients personality, and the major experiences and relationships which make him the person he is.

Barbara Wootton thought,

> It might well be thought that the social worker's best, indeed perhaps her only chance of achieving aims at once so intimate and so ambitious would be to marry her client.[17]

Incidentally, she also took exception to the term 'client', which she thought inappropriate in a social work setting, but her major criticism was,

> The suggestion that complex problems of personal unhappiness or of defiance of social standards can be resolved by a young woman with an academic training in social work is difficult to take seriously.[18]

It was that ability to detect and bring out the weakness of an argument that was also central to Barbara Wootton's style. It did not produce friendly relations with professional organisations or fellow researchers, but Barbara Wootton was not seeking friendship; she was more concerned with wider matters such as promoting the public good. She thought that came from criticism, and criticism led to change. She said in her Autobiography, 'All critics may not be reformers, but all reforms spring from criticism.'[19] In this respect, she saw herself as a conspicuous beneficiary of earlier social critics. That, she said, stopped her being indifferent to her obligations to the future.

The second area in which she made her contribution to criminology was through her involvement in government committees, in particular those that led to the introduction of Community Service Orders. There are few criminologists, or indeed few others, who start with an idea, see it emerge and take shape in a government report, have it introduced and debated in Parliament, watch it be introduced in practice and see it become part of the modern criminal justice system – then watch it taken up internationally and be introduced elsewhere and in other countries, some of which lie outside the common law traditions. Yet this was Barbara Wootton's experience with Community Service Orders. She proposed them, saw their introduction and had the satisfaction of seeing them become part of modern sentencing practice.

The original proposals are found in the Committee on Non Custodial Penalties, which was introduced in 1966. Community Service Orders became operative in 1972. However, the germ of the proposal came to Barbara Wootton in 1961 in Australia when she visited a juvenile court in Alice Springs. Two boys who had stolen money from a church were ordered to spend their weekends for three months volunteering in an old people's home connected to the church. Following this, the idea apparently 'floated into her mind one day on the common sense basis that instead of sending people to prison it would be better to get them to do some useful work'.[20]

In spite of the many criticisms and numerous distortions from the media ('Are you proposing to have convicts working on the roads?'),[21] the Committee accepted the suggestion, and with one or two modifications, Community Service Orders became law. What is surprising is the speed of the process; it went from an idea to a sentence of the court in about a decade, almost unheard of within criminal justice. Barbara Wootton saw the Community Service Order as a success, having what she called a 'maternal instinct' about it, saying, 'This is about the only thing I've got written down in the book I'm going to show St Peter when I get there.'[22] She had more than that, of course, but her comment shows the level of importance she gave this proposal. The long-term results paint a less sanguine picture, and their initial success in reducing crime has waned, but that does not detract from the importance of Barbara Wootton's contribution.

In the second of her influential reports, that on cannabis, the results are less clear cut but no less important. Some of the features of this report were introduced in subsequent legislation in the 1971 Misuse of Drugs Act; others are part of the way we think about drugs. In the 1971 Act, for example, a distinction is made between possession of a prohibited drug for individual use and possession with intent to supply. In the latter, where the amount is seen as more than that for personal use – personal use being regarded as less serious than supply –it avoided the conclusion that possession of whatever amount requires the same level of condemnation. In that Act, substances are classified according to levels of danger, whether to the individual or others, cannabis being a Category B drug, heroin a Category A. Different categories, or 'classes' as they are called, have different sentences available.

It is not so much the individual proposals that were important as the ethos the report created. That is to say, it promoted a more tolerant view of drug use, especially of cannabis use in the climate of the 1960s which was more attuned to what, nowadays, we would call a moral panic. The report was not well received, called by one newspaper 'a junkies charter', and with Barbara Wootton personally selected as the subject of much abuse. Worst of all, the then Home Secretary and later Prime Minister, James Callaghan, referred to the report as being influenced by the 'lobby to legalise cannabis', saying it gave succour to the 'escalation theory', i.e., that soft drug use such as cannabis always led to hard drug use such as heroin. In spite of all the criticisms, the government eventually came round to the view that although cannabis was not to be legalised, then neither was it to be regarded as a 'hard' drug.[23]

The report was a typical Woottonesque report in that it sifted through the available evidence before arriving at a set of conclusions. One wonders what impact on subsequent legislation and drug policy a less reasoned approach might have produced. And what impact would that have had on subsequent crime rates, including rates of convictions and the size of the prison population? The abuse she received from numerous quarters of society when the report was published show what a febrile atmosphere existed at the time. And what a tribute it was to Barbara Wootton's integrity and strength that she pursued a course of action in line with her precepts and beliefs.

Finally, there was her contribution as a criminologist in the House of Lords. This is again difficult to assess, as apart from her influence in the death penalty debate – which was itself hugely important – she was not part of the government, so did not introduce legislation. Yet she spoke on many other topics, including the abolition of corporal punishment in schools, the legalisation of abortion and assisted dying. As a crossbencher, i.e., not attached to a specific political party, she was likely to be seen as an outsider without the backing of a party machine. On the other hand, she had a high public profile as Deputy Speaker, and the first woman to be so appointed, but how much she influenced subsequent legislation is difficult to say. Her own assessment of her performance was typically self-deprecating. She said she 'clocked up an almost unbroken record of failure in my attempts to produce amendments to various Bills'.[24] That may be so, but her contributions were always a model of clarity, and she would surely have been listened to, especially when she spoke on criminal justice and criminology. Her opinions of the House of Lords as a Parliamentary institution were not very flattering, nor were her views of some of the Members. She always insisted that evidence should be produced to support an argument. Apparently some Members were unused to such demands! Small wonder she found speaking in the House of Lords 'difficult'.

In summary, then, Barbara Wootton, as a criminologist, had an important impact on contemporary society. Yet, her contribution to British society in general and criminology in particular seems largely forgotten. She is rarely quoted in the literature nowadays, and rarely acknowledged as an important figure. Her biographer Ann Oakley asks a similar question: 'Why has Barbara Wootton's exceptional contribution to British intellectual and political life been so often forgotten?'[25] And she also asks, 'What might this forgetting tell us about our habits of regarding only certain types of lives as worth remembering?'

Barbara Wootton, the forgotten criminologist?

Her biographer, Ann Oakley, lists three reasons, not necessarily in order of priority or preference, to explain this lack of interest. First, that Barbara

Wootton was a woman, practising her crafts and skills in an otherwise man's world. Second, she was a polymath, and thirdly, she was marginalised in the university system. I want to look at each reason in turn before offering a slightly different perspective.

There is no doubt that in her early years Barbara was the recipient of considerable prejudice, and often in her later years intensely irritated by comments that she 'argued and debated like a man', or had 'a masculine brain'. Certainly, as a woman she experienced considerable discrimination throughout her life, and never ceased to argue that equality of gender was a moral issue which involved a simple judgement: that women should not be discriminated against. As her biographer says, 'That was the beginning and end of the debate'.[26] Yet how much being a woman held her back is difficult to say, although it is highly likely it had an impact. One can think of numerous areas where she was unfairly judged, not the least in her early years by the University of Cambridge, but also by the University of London at Bedford College. The latter discrimination was aided by her choice of academic subjects; criminology, in particular, was a subject taught by men about men.

Barbara complained of the patronising way women were often treated. She listed in her Autobiography[27] some of the idiocies of the then taxation system, which was based on traditional assumptions and the relative incomes of husbands and wives – she earned more than her second husband George, but credits from her income were automatically made to her husband. Even so, I do not think she saw herself as being held back because she was a woman; rather the contrary. She said that 'others broke open the door and I walked through', but that was only part of it; often she broke open the doors by herself.[28] She spoke of the 'measure of her personal debt to purposive social change' that had been brought about by many others, but nowhere said that she herself had been restricted by her gender. On the other hand, she never regarded herself as successful, yet she came out on top in every field in which she moved.

Second, her biographer says she was a polymath. This goes back to the point made in Chapter 1 that being a social scientist was, according to Barbara Wootton, someone who had a licence to trespass, and trespass she certainly did. Her publications and public broadcasts were varied, including debates on the welfare state. She considered specific moral questions such as 'the right to die', as well as writing on law, psychiatry, economics, sociology and criminology. In the Epilogue to her Autobiography, she recognises the dangers of spreading over a wide area, saying, 'My activities have certainly sprawled over many worlds. Had they been more specialized they would perhaps have been more effective' – and for 'effective' we can read 'her position in the scheme of things and posterity'. She adds, however, that 'the sacrifice of wide ranging interests is one which I am temperamentally incapable of making'.[29] She may have been unable to rein in her interests, but these failings have been offset by gains. She aroused that suspicion we have of all polymaths, that they appear insincere, and 'too clever by half' – and sometimes a little dangerous. Ploughing a single furrow seems to produce more approval in the long run.

Thirdly, she was marginalised in the university system. This I think is the most important of her biographer's listed features. Barbara always said she never felt at home in academia, and her experiences at Bedford College must have underlined these feelings. It was a shameful episode, bringing no credit on the college or fellow academics. It also deprived Barbara Wootton of the research funds necessary to develop and promote a research programme. Had this been possible, it is likely that her criminological reputation would have been additionally advanced. Had she been the author of several large-scale longitudinal research studies, her reputation would have been enhanced. She always said policy was dependent on research, and with her fastidious approach to methodological precision, those research documents would have had a lasting imprint. Barbara Wootton always favoured research over, say, the workings and conclusions of Royal Commissions. She thought the findings of Royal Commissions were always overwritten by politicians.

Yet to the reasons given by Barbara Wootton's biographer as to why she is now largely forgotten, I would add others. First, there was something personal about her that was off-putting; namely, that she was basically a loner. This was so not just in the personal sense but intellectually as well. Yet it was consistent with her intellectual approach that she had no need to make way for others, or seek their support. Much of social science research and policy in Britain, as elsewhere, was and still is achieved through social networking. Barbara was not very interested in this.[30] I doubt if there was ever a moment when she sought the company of others in order to advance her career. If she liked you, she would spend time with you; if she didn't, she wouldn't. It was that simple.

She was a difficult person to know, having little of what is called 'small talk', and as she grew older this became increasingly so. Physically tall and imposing, she made people feel uneasy. Sadly, her likeability decreased as she got older, a fact of which she was well aware.[31] Whether she was sufficiently concerned about these personal qualities or wanted to do something about them is difficult to say; she certainly complained about being lonely, but like many in that situation did little to become more sociable. It is interesting that she did little to develop close family ties, whether with her surviving brother, his children or other family members. She kept close ties with Vera Seal and one or two other friends, but not, it seems, with near or distant family – but she did keep in touch with some of Jack's family. And incidentally, there was no doubt that Jack Wootton continued to retain an epic and eponymic presence through it all. He may have taken up a small proportion of Barbara Wootton's life in a physical sense, but one suspects he was always there, influencing her in some way.

Nor were her views presented in ways aimed at establishing a rapport. I have said of her style of writing that her views were regularly presented in terms of a biting wit, and sometimes an equally biting sarcasm. Take for example that critique of social casework, which she described as involving the social worker as the emotionally detached helper dealing with the emotionally involved client thrashing about in his emotional turmoil.[32] It was not an approach aimed at building bridges, mending fences or promoting friendships.

There is no evidence that she ever collaborated with anyone or sought out friendships aimed at advancing her career. The closest we get to seeing any sort of collaboration was in *Social Science and Social Pathology*, where she said she was 'Assisted by Vera Seal and Rosalind Chambers'. Yet this was hardly collaboration; Vera Seal acted only as a research assistant, providing papers, articles in journals and other published works. Rosalind Chambers only wrote Appendix 2, entitled 'Professionalism in social work'. In the Preface, Barbara confirmed that 'the actual text of the book has been put together entirely by myself'. She never collaborated because she was self-sufficient, confident of the correctness of her approach and prepared to be responsible for what she said. On the other hand, I doubt very much if there were many who would have wanted to collaborate with her; it would have been a difficult exercise and too much to ask or expect her to compromise or seek another point of view. Once her mind was made up, that was it. She said what she thought was correct and was confident in doing so. She was sufficiently assured in her own ability to know how best to proceed, and did not need others to assist her.

When she said sociology was 'a load of waffle' and theoretical sociology 'bunk', she did not expect to endear herself to other sociologists.[33] Some senior social scientists saw such comments as limiting her accomplishments, but her biographer says she never worried about upsetting people. It was a strength if one wants to see it that way, but a weakness too. When she said she wanted to build a better world, she should not have expected to do so alone; she needed assistance from others, especially from like-minded fellow travellers. Upsetting them would not help her cause. If she did not bother with them, she could not expect them to bother with her.

Thirdly, I suggest there was an element of parochialism in her writings. That is to say, there was no strong international appeal, except perhaps in common law countries. She was often concerned with such questions as the nature of legal responsibility, or the role of psychiatry within the legal system, or the development of the juvenile court. But these were British considerations, and would have a limited interest outside common law jurisdictions. In this sense, she has been left behind by events. Criminology is now a worldwide enterprise, having long since moved from its common law dominance, and questions of common law interest have inevitably become more peripheral. Criminology is now an international subject; it is difficult to ignore the international dimension of say, a study of substance abuse, or of slavery or of cybercrime.

And even within those parochial boundaries, there has been a fragmentation of British criminology as an academic discipline, which means that the questions Barbara Wootton asked have become less dominant. Peripheral matters have assumed more importance, so that questions about the role of the courts, or the ethical dimension of punishment or mental health matters within the jurisdiction of the courts, are given less consideration. We are more interested in the developments of the subject itself than the legal questions surrounding the crime.

Finally, she founded no school, nor did she promote or produce any new theory. Rather, she was a breaker of images, a loner, an empiricist and a Utilitarian who sought only that which would lead to improvements, even if doing so meant being destructive in her criticisms. As such, she did not fit the fashionable mould of the theoretician who was concerned to develop the theory for its own sake. To emphasise an earlier point: Barbara Wootton was seeking to promote the public good, and there is little in the later form of criminology which now approximates that. Perhaps here lies the explanation as to why she is not considered nowadays; she is out of touch and out of fashion. Her form of criminology is no longer interesting, exciting or in keeping with the spirit of the times. She was a product of her era; modern criminology reflects the later version.

There was a second question asked by Barbara's biographer: 'what might this forgetting tell us about our habits of regarding only certain types of lives as worth remembering?' Is it that we don't remember women as readily as we remember men? And is it that women's achievements are considered less worthy of commendation than those of men – unless of course one can see some deep struggle at work, such as in the case of the suffragettes? In Barbara's case, there wasn't; she was too clever, too privileged and too confident for that. The personal tragedy of her early life was long ago and of another age. Or, is it that we don't remember women criminologists, criminology being what it always was, a masculine subject where men talk about men?

Or perhaps it has nothing to do with gender, and is more that in Britain, intellectuals (alongside those in business and engineers) and other pointed-headed people are rarely honoured, with preference given to others such as actors and those playing sports? Perhaps so. There has always been a deep distrust in Britain of intellectuals, and they are regarded as unstable and unworldly, steeped in ivory and out of touch with the real world. The 'University of Life' is said to provide more wisdom than can be found in any book. There is a long list of aphorisms displaying the dangers of too much learning and of its long-term effects on one's sanity. Barbara might not be regarded as unstable, unworldly or whatever, but her politics and second marriage suggested she might be slightly odd. And sometimes her judgement was seriously unsound, as when she claimed that the socialist form of organisation in Russia under Stalin in the 1930s was to be preferred as being more efficient and more humane than one run for private profit.[34] The press was very interested in her marriage to George when they saw a university don was marrying a taxi driver, and thought that was newsworthy, but only because of the social distance between them. It was not her intellectual contribution to criminology or society that mattered.

Barbara Wootton was too serious to be a public entertainer, although she was a public figure. She broadcast regularly on *The Brains Trust* and other like BBC radio programmes, and was also a frequent letter writer to *The Times*, but her contributions were always on serious topics. She spoke of public policy and of the public good, of being a public servant and of moral questions, such as the unequal distribution of wealth. (She also wrote to *The Times* about the morality of politicians, saying that extramarital affairs should not be a cause for resignation. 'If impeccable marital fidelity is to be made a condition of political office it should be explicitly stated at the outset' (26 May 1973).) And although by inclination she never wanted to be part of the Establishment, she was nonetheless an Establishment figure. In short, perhaps it was because she was a one-off, and belonged nowhere, or rather was not easy to pigeonhole in the scheme of things. Perhaps this helps explain why she is no longer remembered. Upper class, intelligent ladies who were serious rather than frivolous rarely make the news, and Barbara was one of those.

It is possible to see Barbara Wootton as, in some small way, the architect of her own demise. David Downes thinks her trenchant criticism helped usher in a far more adventurous phase of criminology which was out of place with her way of thinking.[35] Yet her form of criminology emphasised empiricism, which did not fit with the spirit of later times. As I said earlier, the more flamboyant theories of the 1960s, such as labelling theory, or those surrounding ethnomethodology which eschewed a statistical analysis, were seen as more exciting than an empiricism which slowly added to knowledge. It is possible to regard Barbara Wootton as simply on the wrong side of history, in the sense that her world has passed away. All of this suggests that the later version of criminology was in a different world from the aspirations of *Testament for Social Science*, with its hopes for a steady accumulation of knowledge based on an established positivist methodology. She always thought the statistician would have the last word in any evaluation of a particular theory. Later criminologists asked different questions and sought different answers.

Other changes were taking place which Barbara Wootton could not have predicted, and of which she would not approve. She could not have predicted or wanted a situation whereby criminology has sometimes become a vehicle for a political cause, or some crusading think tank. Nor would she have wanted to be involved in identity politics, where social science is used to advance the position of selected social groups. Barbara Wootton would not have approved of these ways in which social science is being transformed, or rather used. Her brand of social science was in direct lineage from that of its early founders, Comte, Mill and Spencer, and from the earnest social accounting of the Webbs.[36] She was in the tradition of C. Wright Mills (or C. Wright Mills was in the tradition of Barbara Wootton), who was also concerned to remove the value-laden assumptions that masqueraded as knowledge in professional utterances. Not for Barbara Wootton were the claims of celebrities or of special interest groups; her methodology was of a different order.[37]

Of course, Barbara Wootton fought her own political causes, the abolition of the death penalty being the most obvious, and in this sense was doing no more than those of the identity criminologists of the 21st century. The difference, however, is one of degree, ably put by C. Wright Mills, who said 'Social research of any kind is advanced by ideas: it is only disciplined by fact.'[38] Identity social science or the celebritisation of social problems omits the importance of those 'facts', and this is the essential difference. As I said before, Barbara Wootton was keen on facts, which provided evidence as the basis of all scientific enquiry and without which criminology could not advance.

Some concluding comments

It is against this background that Barbara Wootton made her contribution to British criminology. In some ways she was lucky, in that it is perhaps easier to make one's mark when there is little competition, but in other ways more difficult. As a lone figure, she had few shoulders on which to climb, and few colleagues to turn to when seeking help. But then Barbara rarely needed shoulders or colleagues to turn to for help. She was self-sufficient, confident and comfortable in what she was doing.

As with all of us, there are periods or events which shape our lives, and in Barbara's case I think there were three; the first and most obvious was Jack's death. How different would things have been had he lived? There would have been a different Barbara Wootton, perhaps someone who would have been less iconoclastic, and likely also to have been interested in different things, perhaps other than criminology. She would most likely have taken a different path. Or perhaps, had her second marriage worked, Barbara would have been also involved in a domestic routine, and with children, her life and outlook might also have been different. Again, she may have been less interested in criminology and more interested in other matters, perhaps more closely related to international affairs, or family life and family welfare. Finally, there was that period at Bedford College. Had this turned out as she wished, and had she been the architect of large-scale social surveys, she would have had colleagues with whom she could discuss and data to examine. Sadly, the debacle there ruled that out. She was left with other ways to make her contribution.

Her biographer says not many people thought Barbara Wootton was afraid of anything, but there was an intense vulnerability about her that was not readily apparent.[39] She greatly disliked being alone, which grew worse as she got older. She arranged for her friend Vera Seal to have a chair and table in the Chelsea juvenile court so that she could be with someone she was close to throughout the proceedings. She was surprisingly quite shy, finding social events quite difficult.

As Barbara grew older, Vera played an increasingly important part in her life, being her constant friend and companion. Barbara was lucky in having someone as devoted as Vera. The devotion was deep and sincere; it was said in Vera's obituary that she died with a photograph of Barbara above her head, and a book written by Barbara in her hand. There is no doubt that Vera helped Barbara through the latter years of Barbara's life, and without Vera, Barbara would have been less independent and more lonely. It was sad therefore that in Barbara's last months she was unable to appreciate the help and assistance given by Vera, and noble of Vera that her affection for Barbara remained during that difficult period.

If there were vulnerabilities, they were not publicly displayed. Barbara's upbringing never allowed for public displays of emotion, whether of happiness or grief. From that upper-middle-class Edwardian background, displays of public emotion were simply not considered, so that when Jack died the aim was to get on with things and keep one's grief to oneself. In her public persona, the veneer of unemotional superrationality was all important. She did not go in for emotional displays; the intellect was the most important.

Barbara suffered for many years from what she called 'prolonged periods of great emotional disturbance', which she kept going with the help of modern antidepressant drugs. She would not of course calls these periods 'depressions' – that was too much of an acceptance of psychiatric influence for her liking – but surely these are what they were. Her father and brother were similarly afflicted, and it is highly probable that Barbara followed the family in this respect.[40] Of course, she kept these episodes to herself, or to a very small circle of very close friends.

We need also to remember her contributions in subjects other than criminology, particularly in economics and social policy/social welfare. I do not want to dwell too much on this, as it lies outside this field of enquiry, but it needs to be underlined that Barbara Wootton was well regarded as an economist, as she was in other areas of social science. In recognition of her contribution to economics, half of her *Festschrift* was given over to that, including planning and social welfare. In these early publications, we can see elements of a later more recognisable Wootton-type style. In *Lament*, for example, there is that pithy remark, now famous, that 'Wherever six economists are gathered there are seven opinions.'[41] Her books on economics have a familiar theme: economics must be tested against empirical data, a point well made in *Lament* and repeated in various forms throughout. Her view, as stated in *Lament*, was that economics as then taught was defective in the following respects: it was of no practical use, it was unintelligible to the plain man, it was riddled with and weakened by internal disputes, it ignored reality, and at its heart it was an elaborate system of apologetics for capitalism. No wonder her biographer said it was 'not a polite book'.[42]

She wrote too of social policy and of more general matters, such as the Beveridge Report and the conditions of the welfare state. She also wrote a novel, but this apparently was not well received. Novels did not suit her style; they were too stilted and formal – this unlike the carefully framed prose of her other writings, which make her style readable and easily recognised.

She had her blind spots, of course. She was for some years a member of the Visiting Committee at Holloway Prison for Women,[43] yet as I said a number of times, she said little about the plight of women prisoners. During her period as a Visitor, prisoners in Holloway were often overprescribed powerful psychiatric tranquilisers and given psychiatric diagnoses reducing them to patients, when more often than not they were prisoners feeling the pains of their imprisonment. There were also inadequate mother and baby facilities at Holloway during that period, and yet Barbara made no comment on this.

How would Barbara Wootton want to be remembered, or rather what would she want to be remembered for? As an economist, sociologist, criminologist or what? She disliked labels, so perhaps just as a social scientist. She often referred to herself in those terms. Although she said she was no longer interested in economics, she returned to it time and again. It was, after all, her first interest. But it is doubtful that she wished to be remembered as an economist. Her *Lament* suggested that she thought there were too many blind alleys in economics to interest her, although David Whynes in the *Festschrift* suggests economics has experienced enormous changes in the subject over the last few years.[44] That might not be enough for Barbara Wootton.

It is doubtful that she would like to be remembered as an academic, although she clearly had a strong academic leaning. She was not comfortable as an academic in a university setting. She said she disliked the squabbling and the disputes over petty matters and the administrative demands placed on her, although she spent 13 years at Bedford College with the title of Professor conferred in 1948. Incidentally, she had little time for journalists, believing the gulf between the social scientist and journalist was unbridgeable. 'Scientific observation and the journalist is as oil and water.'[45]

Nor would she wish to be remembered as a peer in the House of Lords. She thought no one in their right senses would invent the present House if it did not already exist, adding that no tears would be shed by her if their Lordships were destined to lose their legislative powers.[46] It was, she thought, a comfortable place in which to reside – she thought about 10% of Members were asleep during the sittings. She clearly enjoyed certain aspects of the House, the conviviality, the status coming from the title and the pleasant and interesting conversation. She thought also in the words of Iolanthe, 'they might do nothing in particular but they do it very well'. Nonetheless, her conclusion was, 'Not surprisingly, in spite of all the glamour with which their Lordships' proceedings are invested, this game at playing at deciding things which are really decided somewhere else tends to pall after a time.'[47]

One suspects that when Barbara Wootton spoke of criminology, this was new to many Members. She was seen to be offering a new and important perspective. Her insistence on 'evidence' was certainly new to some in the late postwar period, although to others it was a welcome inclusion. She gave a great deal of her time to the House, and it was strange therefore that she felt that overall she had little influence. She questioned the 'right of their Lordships to exist at all', and questioned too the way the press was preoccupied with trivialities, especially when it concerned female speakers, who she said were particularly vulnerable.[48] Her conclusion: 'No, clearly I am not cut out to be a good Parliamentarian,'[49] but this surely is too modest. She would not have been invited to be a Deputy Speaker otherwise.

If not academe or the House of Lords, what then? I suspect the answer is that she would wish to be remembered for her contribution to criminology. I suspect criminology was where she felt most at home, supplemented of course through her experiences as a magistrate. And in the field of criminology, I suspect she would wish to be remembered most for her contribution to those Reports on Cannabis and Non Custodial Penalties, followed closely by her book *Social Science and Social Pathology*, with *Testament for Social Science* not far behind. Nor should we forget the Hamlyn Lectures and *Crime and Penal Policy*, although the latter two books were more of a commentary on events than groundbreaking publications. Nonetheless, they were considerable achievements, if only for the debate on criminal responsibility.

So, in conclusion, it seems it is as a criminologist that Barbara Wootton should be remembered, and a pioneering one at that.

Notes

1 Oakley A (2011) *A Critical Woman*. Bloomsbury Academic p. 346.
2 Wootton B (1950) *Testament for Social Science*. George Allen and Unwin p. 6.
3 Wootton B (1967) *In a World I Never Made. Autobiographical Reflections*. George Allen and Unwin p. 21.
4 Ibid. p. 210.
5 One public figure in the 1950s who called himself a criminologist was Edgar Lustgarten, but his books and lectures were mainly on notable criminal cases and the police attempts to solve them with trials; and courtroom procedures that followed criminology, in the public mind, according to Lustgarten, was of a series of murder cases and the subsequent convictions. It was not about

the way offenders were managed in the criminal justice system or about them as offenders.

6 Wootton B (1967) *In a World I Never Made. Autobiographical Reflections*. George Allen and Unwin. op. cit. p. 210.
7 Ibid. p. 81.
8 Downes D. (1986) Back to basics: Reflections on Barbara Wootton's 'twelve criminological hypotheses'. In Bean PT and Whynes D (eds) *Barbara Wootton. Social Science and Public Policy. Essays in her Honour*. Tavistock p. 213.
9 Wootton B (1967) *In a World I Never Made. Autobiographical Reflections*. George Allen and Unwin. op. cit. p. 210.
10 Barbara's one and only criminal conviction was as a motoring offender! She was fined 10 shillings for speeding in Regents Park London. Apparently, she was hurrying home to hear one of her broadcasts. It is not clear if she was offering this as a defence or a mitigating circumstance, but it shows how the mighty can fall. She became another of those 'typical modern offenders', but unlike many others in this category was not a recidivist.
11 Smith J (1986) Responsibility in criminal law. In Bean PT and Whynes D (eds) *Barbara Wootton. Social Science and Public Policy. Essays in her Honour*. Tavistick p. 141.
12 Oakley A (2011) *A Critical Woman*. Bloomsbury Academic. op. cit. p. 290.
13 Wootton B (1967) *In a World I Never Made. Autobiographical Reflections*. George Allen and Unwin. op. cit. p. 279.
14 Ibid. p. 217.
15 Wootton B (1959) *Social Science and Social Pathology*. George Allen and Unwin p. 228.
16 Ibid. p. 278.
17 Ibid. p. 273.
18 Ibid. p. 274.
19 Wootton B (1967) *In a World I Never Made. Autobiographical Reflections*. George Allen and Unwin. op. cit. p. 279.
20 Oakley A (2011) *A Critical Woman*. Bloomsbury Academic. op. cit. p. 272.
21 Ibid. p. 274.
22 Ibid. p. 276.
23 Ibid. p. 268.
24 Wootton B (1978) *Crime and Penal Policy; Reflections on Fifty Years Experience*. Allen and Unwin p. 17.
25 Oakley A (2011) *A Critical Woman*. Bloomsbury Academic. op. cit. pp. 1–2.
26 Ibid. p. 5.
27 Ibid. Chapter 6.
28 See also Aldridge M (1986) An organising female with a briefcase. In Bean PT and Whynes D (eds) *Barbara Wootton. Social Science and Public Policy. Essays in her Honour*. Tavistock pp. 40–56.
29 Wootton B (1967) *In a World I Never Made. Autobiographical Reflections*. George Allen and Unwin. op. cit. p. 278.
30 Oakley A (2011) *A Critical Woman*. Bloomsbury Academic. op. cit. p. 353.
31 Ibid. p. 356.
32 Wootton B (1959) *Social Science and Social Pathology*. George Allen and Unwin. op. cit. p. 281.
33 Ibid. p. 346.

34 Wootton B (1967) *In a World I Never Made. Autobiographical Reflections.* George Allen and Unwin. op. cit. Her visit to Russia is reported in her Autobiography pp. 78–82, and one comment made by her hosts remained with Barbara forever: 'So, you come from England where they beat children' (p. 78). Hence her opposition to corporal punishment in schools.

35 Downes D (1986) Back to basics: Reflections on Barbara Wootton's 'twelve criminological hypotheses'. In Bean PT and Whynes D (eds) *Barbara Wootton. Social Science and Public Policy. Essays in her Honour.* Tavistock. op. cit. p. 212.

36 Oakley A (2011) A *Critical Woman*. Bloomsbury Academic. op. cit. pp. 347–348.

37 Take for example studies of human trafficking. Here, much of the literature is distorted by those seeking a particular political and moral agenda. One criminologist claims that in no other area of the social sciences has ideology contaminated knowledge more pervasively than in the writings of human trafficking, especially that related to the sex industry. This is especially so where the data is provided by organisations and celebrities who have an interest in funding their selected projects. These warnings come most directly from a paper by Ronald Weitzer (2014), who challenges many of the basic assumptions on which the popular image of trafficking rests, i.e., that the number of trafficking victims worldwide is huge, that the magnitude of trafficking is steadily growing worldwide, that human trafficking is the second- or third-largest organised criminal enterprise in the world after illegal drug- and weapons-trading, and that sex trafficking is more prevalent and/or more serious than labour trafficking (note 50). Many reports, he says, are based on flawed national data and do not meet the accepted canons of scientific enquiry. He also says few are conducted as empirical studies, mostly recirculating anecdotal or sensationalist information.

Add to this the claims by Dina Haynes, who talks of the 'celebritization' of human trafficking. She says the literature on human trafficking is susceptible to alluring and sensational narratives, providing an ideal platform for the celebrity-as-rescuer. For not only does the celebrity receive media attention, much of course to the benefit of the celebrity, but also the organisation the celebrity represents. It matters little that the claims to knowledge or expertise are insignificant; the aim of celebrity endorsement is not to provide facts, but to make a visceral appeal. The primary drawbacks of celebrity activism are the superficial and uninformed narratives they provide, and the lack of accountability for the solutions they propose.

38 Wright MC (1959) *The Sociological Imagination*. Oxford University Press p. 71.

39 Oakley A (2011) A *Critical Woman*. Bloomsbury Academic. op. cit. p. 355.

40 Ibid. p. 355.

41 Ibid. p. 166.

42 Ibid. p. 161.

43 Wootton B (1978) *Crime and Penal Policy; Reflections on Fifty Years Experience*. Allen and Unwin. op. cit. p. 18.

44 Whynes D (1986) Is economics still lamentable? In Bean PT and Whynes D (eds) *Barbara Wootton. Social Science and Public Policy. Essays in her Honour.* Tavistock p. 72.

45 Wootton B (1967) *In a World I Never Made. Autobiographical Reflections.* George Allen and Unwin. op. cit. p. 275.

46 Ibid. pp. 273–274.
47 Ibid. pp. 272–273.
48 Ibid. p. 270.
49 Ibid. p. 2.

References for publications by Barbara Wootton

A more complete list of Barbara Wootton's publications can be found in Seal V and Bean P.T. (1992) (eds) *Barbara Wootton. Selected Writings*. MacMillan Vols 1–4.

Wootton B (1950) *Testament for Social Science*. George Allen and Unwin.

Wootton B (1959) *Social Science and Social Pathology*. George Allen and Unwin.

Wootton B (1962) A *Social Scientists Approach to Maternal Deprivation in Deprivation of Maternal Care; A Reassessment of Its Effects*. WHO pp. 63–73.

Wootton B (1963) *Crime and the Criminal Law: Reflections of a Magistrate and a Social Scientist* (The Hamlyn Lectures) Stevens and Sons. (Second Edition 1981 with postscripts to each chapter).

Wootton B (1967) *In a World I Never Made. Autobiographical Reflections*. George Allen and Unwin.

Wootton B (1972) Crime responsibility and prevention. Reprinted In Gerber R and McAnany D (eds) *Contemporary Punishment*. University of Notre Dame Press pp. 164–175.

Wootton B (1978) *Crime and Penal Policy; Reflections on Fifty Years Experience*. Allen and Unwin.

Wootton B (1992) The Administration of justice. Lecture given to the University of Leeds. Reprinted In Seal V and Bean P (eds) *Barbara Wootton Selected Writings Vol. 1 Crime and the Penal System* pp. 95–108.

Wootton B. (1992) Some reflections on the first five years of community service. Reprinted In Seal V and Bean P (eds) *Barbara Wootton Selected Writings Vol. 1 Crime and the Penal System* pp. 143–145.

Wootton B (1992) Who are the criminals? Reprinted In Seal V and Bean P (eds) *Barbara Wootton Selected Writings Vol. 1 Crime and the Penal System* pp. 109–117.

Wootton B (1992) Time and the drug scene. Reprinted In Seal V and Bean P (eds) *Barbara Wootton Selected Writings Vol. 1 Crime and the Penal System* pp. 135–137.

Wootton B (1992) Sickness or sin? Reprinted In Seal V and Bean P (eds) *Barbara Wootton Selected Writings Vol. 2 Crime and the Penal System* pp. 76–84.

Wootton B (1992) The law, the doctor and the deviant. Reprinted In Seal V and Bean P (eds) *Barbara Wootton Selected Writings Vol. 2 Crime and the Penal System* pp. 61–75.

Wootton B (1992) Psychiatry ethics and the law. Reprinted In Seal V and Bean P (eds) *Barbara Wootton Selected Writings Vol. 2 Crime and the Penal System* pp. 1–12.

Index

Adam, Adele (nee Kensington) 2–3
Adam, Arthur 2, 4
Adam, James 2, 5
Adam, Neil 2, 4
adult education *see* Morley College
Advisory Council on the Penal System 18
Aldridge, M. 22, 123
American Bar Association 69–70
Athenaeum, The 16
Autobiography of Barbara Wootton *see end of each chapter*

BBC 16–17, 117
Bean, Philip 54, 77; with Seal, Vera 60, 76, 77, 101, 102; with Whynes, David 102 123, 124
Bedford College 10–11, 114, 119
Bentham, Jeremy 39, 41
biography of Barbara Wootton *see* Oakley, Ann
Blom-Cooper, Louis 38, 53
Bowlby thesis, the 28–29, 33, 35, 52, 74, 88
broken homes 33

Callaghan, James 63, 66
Cambridge University 6, 19
Cannabis Report 18, 60–67, 75, 111
casework, social *see* social work
Children's Panels, in Scotland 46–47
collective conscience *see* Durkheim, Emile
Community Service Order 67–72, 75; contribution of 100–111; defined 69–70; failure rate of 70–71; net widening of 71; supervision of 71–72
Companion of Honour 19
compulsory admissions to mental hospitals 100
Comte, Auguste 11, 118
courts 36–38
crime, extent of 56, 60; *see also Chapter 3 passim*

day fines 72–73
death penalty, debate on 11–12
Devlin, Lord 94
Downes, David 32, 34–35, 36, 53, 107, 118, 123, 124
Durkheim, Emile 43–44, 54

Eugenics Society 30

female criminality 57–58
Festchrift see Bean, Philip; Whynes, David
Fyval, T. 76

Girton College, Cambridge 4, 6, 7
Glueck, Sheldon and Eleanor 34
Goffman, Irving 35–36, 53
Gruenhut, Max 106–107

Hamlyn Lectures *see* Oakley, Ann
Hart, Herbert 53, 93, 98, 103; *see also* Wootton-Hart debate

Hedderman, Carol 72
Hospital Order under Mental Health Act 102
Hough, Michael 72

Jenkins, Roy 68
Johnson, Yvonne 82, 101
judges, appointment of 37–38
jury system 38
just deserts 39–40
juvenile court 45–48; *see also* Youth Courts
juvenile delinquents 5–6, 64

labelling theory 35, 107
Labour Party 7, 19
legal responsibility defined 94
Lords, House of, debates 11–12, 80, 112, 121
Lustgarten, Edgar 122

MacPherson, Stewart 23
magistrate, Barbara Wootton as 9, 36, 37–39
Mair, George 48–49, 54
maladjusted persons, defined 88
McGregor, Lord 23
McNaughton Rules 89, 102
McWilliams, Bill 70, 77
mens rea, debate on 93–95
mental health: defined 86; responsibility with 85–86, 89, 91
mentally abnormal offender *see Chapter 4 passim*
Mill, John Stuart 11, 64, 66, 105, 118
Miller, Emanuel 106–107
Mills, C. Wright 118, 124
Milton, Sir Frank 70
Morley College 7–8
Morris, Norval 69, 71, 74, 77, 78
motoring offenders 9–10, 58–60

Nuffield Foundation 13

Oakley, Ann 9, 23–25, 52, 54, 55, 68–69, 77, 78, 101, 102, 112, 122, 123, 124

Parliamentary debates 50; on corporal punishment in schools 50; on death penalty 50–51; on drug offenders 60–67
parole supervision 72
Pease, Ken 70, 77
penal system 48–50
Petersilia, Joan 71
Prison Reform Trust 54
Probation Advisory Committee 17
probation service 48–49, 69; statistics of 84
problem family 30–31, 35
psychiatry, influence of 34; in criminal justice 91–92; *see also Chapter 4 passim*
Psychiatry, Royal College of 19
psychopathy: defined 34; as a form of mental disorder 89–90

Radzinowicz, Sir Leon 106–107
reports, to the courts 42–43; *see also* sentencing
responsibility 85, 89–93, 122; *see also Chapter 4 passim*
Royal Commission on the Penal System 17–18; members of 22

scientific method, in social science 11–12, 106–107, *Chapter 5 passim*; approach to sentencing 42–45; value of 41
Seal, Vera 15, 20, 60, 115, 119; *see also* Bean, Philip
Sellin, Thorsten 51–52
sentencing 39–45; aims of 40–41; defects of present system 40–41; and *mens rea* 97; *see also* scientific method, in social science, approach to sentencing
Smith, John 22, 96, 98, 102, 103–108, 123
social casework *see* social work
social enquiry reports 42–43; *see also* reports, to the courts
social pathology 27–30
social work: defined 80–81; relationships with clients 81–82; treatment given 81–82; *see also Chapter 2 passim*

stop and search 67
Streatfeild Committee 17, 36, 41–42, 54, 55, 61
strict liability offences 94–95
subcultural theory 35
Sutherland, Edwin 107
Szasz, Thomas 86–87, 88, 92

tariff 41, 70; *see also* sentencing
Tonry, Michael 69, 71, 74, 77, 78
'Twelve criminological hypotheses' 31–36

Utilitarian 2, 39; *see also* scientific method, in social science

Webster, R. 77
Weitzer, R. 124
Whynes, David 23–24, 102, 121, 123, 124; *see also* Bean, Philip
Willett, Trevor 58–59
women offenders 48, 121
Wootton, Barbara: early years 2–7; final years 20–21; legacy *Chapter 5 passim*; as woman 7, 113, 116
Wootton-Hart debate 93–95
Wootton, Jack 4–5, 115, 119
Wright, George 8–9, 15, 119

young offenders *see* juvenile court
Youth Courts *see* juvenile court

For Product Safety Concerns and Information please contact our EU
representative GPSR@taylorandfrancis.com
Taylor & Francis Verlag GmbH, Kaufingerstraße 24, 80331 München, Germany

www.ingramcontent.com/pod-product-compliance
Ingram Content Group UK Ltd.
Pitfield, Milton Keynes, MK11 3LW, UK
UKHW022023061126
477531UK00002B/7
* 9 7 8 0 3 6 7 2 5 3 9 6 7 *